5/5/12

AF594193

To Jo,

Super nurse, wonderful friend who was kind enough to share her terrific daughter with me for a year. Thanks so much for helping to "Strike Out" Huntington's.

Carol McKechnie Montgomery

'The Deacon's' Daughter

'Daddy's girl' relives her life

With Hall of Fame Baseball Manager

Bill McKechnie

By Carol McKechnie Montgomery

with

Jerry Hanks

ISBN 0-7414-6811-5

Printed in the United States of America

Published September 2011

INFINITY PUBLISHING
1094 New DeHaven Street, Suite 100
West Conshohocken, PA 19428-2713
Toll-free (877) BUY BOOK
Local Phone (610) 941-9999
Fax (610) 941-9959
Info@buybooksontheweb.com
www.buybooksontheweb.com

Contents

DEDICATION

This book is dedicated to all persons and their families who have been challenged with the devastation of Huntington's Disease, which claimed the life of my first husband, Don, and which now afflicts my son Scott. Let us pray that with God's help a cure can soon be found.

ACKNOWLEDGMENTS

This book would never have been possible without the endearing and enduring support of my family and especially my husband Ted and my friend Darlene Short and her daughter Jennifer, who kept telling me, "You should write a book."

Also worthy of note in making this book a reality is my ghostwriter, Jerry Hanks, and his friend, Bob Davis, a graphic artist, and Bob's assistant, Rebecca English, who designed the cover and also formatted the inside pages of the book along with the many photographs.

To all of them and to all others whose names are mentioned in the pages which follow, I owe my heartfelt gratitude.

Carol Montgomery
Jacksonville, Florida

INTRODUCTION

What prompts someone to write an autobiography? I never really gave it much thought. But if someone had ever asked me, I suppose I would have answered that most autobiographies are ego trips. Not so with me.

"'The Deacon's' Daughter" is self-preservation in a double sense. First, it provides my children and grandchildren with memories of me as their mother and grandmother, and it also lets me tell them what it was like to grow up as the daughter of baseball legend Bill McKechnie. And, second, it will stop my husband Ted from asking me every week, "When are you starting your book?"

I knew my fate was sealed when Ted came home from a Rotary Club meeting one day and told me that one of his fellow Rotarians was a writer/ghostwriter and editor – and also, by his own admission, was a baseball nerd who belonged to the Society for American Baseball Research.

A week later, Jerry Hanks showed up at our house, armed with a legal pad and pencil, and started asking me questions. After that, he couldn't shut me up. He made it all so easy and the stories started pouring out of me.

After an hour's worth of scribbles, Jerry would leave and return a week or so later with a chapter for me to review and approve. I really made very few changes. Everything I rambled about, Jerry always managed to reduce to written form and I felt like, "Yeah, that's just what I wanted to say."

Now, it's a year later and here, for your enjoyment and, I hope, for the enjoyment of my children, grandchildren and my husband Ted, is "'The Deacon's' Daughter" – and what it *really* was like to grow up as the daughter of Bill McKechnie.

1

Baseball's Baby

How many little girls are lucky enough to have had as playmates some of the best known baseball players of their time? How many are lucky enough to have frolicked in the sun for a month every year at a spring training site in Florida or Arizona?

Dad's plaque at the National Baseball Hall of Fame in Cooperstown, New York, where Dad was enshrined in 1962.

I did. Those were just a few of the perks of growing up as the youngest daughter of Hall of Fame Baseball Manager Bill McKechnie.

When my husband Ted and I meet people today, the conversation sometimes drifts around to baseball and we may ask, "Have you ever heard of Bill McKechnie?" That usually produces either a blank stare or the honest admission, "I don't think I've ever heard of him."

I suppose that's understandable. Dad passed away in 1965 and he was inducted into Baseball's Hall of Fame three years before that as the only manager ever to lead three different teams to National League pennants and two of them to World Series championships.

When I tell people today that I'm Bill McKechnie's daughter and tell them when he died, I know they must be thinking, "That's impossible. Maybe I misunderstood. Carol must mean she is Bill McKechnie's *granddaughter.*"

No. I'm his daughter. You see Dad was 46 years old when I was born and my mother was 44. I was born in Pittsburgh but grew up in suburban Wilkinsburg, which was Dad's hometown and a place I love to this day.

Baseball? The memories grow more cherished with each passing year.

1928 B.C. (Before Carol). In shirt and tie Dad sits in the sand at Pass-a-Grille Beach in Florida with Mother, my sister Bea, my older brother Bill and my younger brother Jim. Where was I? I wasn't even a dream in 1928. The picture was taken during spring training and Dad went on to lead the St. Louis Cardinals to the National League pennant.

My earliest recollection dates back to when I was maybe three or four years old and I remember being in St. Petersburg for spring training. Dad – or Daddy as I always called him when the two of us were together – was the manager of the Boston Braves. We stayed at the West Coast Inn, across the bay from Tampa and within walking distance of Al Lang Field.

I wasn't aware of it at the time, but Dad had already managed the Pittsburgh Pirates to a World Series title in 1925 and the St. Louis Cardinals to the National League pennant in 1928.

Now Dad was manager of the Braves and the players were all so nice to me. We all stayed at the same hotel and one of my favorites was a catcher named Al Spohrer. He was bald and very self-conscious about it. When he'd chase a popup behind home plate, he'd flip off his mask but somehow his hat never came off his head along with the mask. Don't ask me how he did it. All that mattered to me was that he'd sometimes take me to the beach and let me play in the water. I loved that.

Rabbit Maranville, who also is in the Hall of Fame, was another favorite of mine. Rabbit played shortstop for the Cardinals when Dad managed the team to the pennant in 1928. Now Rabbit was nearing the end of his playing career but what I remember was how much fun it was playing hide-and-seek with him in the lobby of the hotel.

And then there was my love affair with Catcher Al Lopez. To avoid being struck by a foul ball, Mother and I always sat behind the screen behind home plate. When an inning ended, Al would take off his mask and stare up at me as he walked toward the dugout. And I would stare back, peering into his eyes. He promised he would "wait for me." Well, things didn't work out quite that way. But Al did OK. He was inducted into the Hall of Fame in 1977 and led the Cleveland Indians to the American League pennant in 1954 and did the same thing five years later with the Chicago White Sox.

Al Lang, for whom the spring training field was named, was a friend of Dad's going all the way back to their days together in Pennsylvania, when Mr. Lang owned and operated a laundry in Pittsburgh known as Brace Brothers. As a boy growing up, Dad drove a horse-drawn laundry truck for Mr. Lang. Then they went their separate ways. Mr. Lang moved to Florida and became mayor of St. Petersburg and was largely responsible for bringing spring training and the Grapefruit League to Florida.

Dad became a professional baseball player and manager and now they were together again. Mr. Lang was about 6-foot-4 and skinny and I always referred to him as "the Old Buzzard" (in a very kindly way). He and his wife Marie had no children and I was like their grandchild. When Mr. Lang died he left me $500 in his will, which was a lot of money in those days.

Another one of my early childhood favorites was Umpire Bill Stewart. The umpires also stayed at the West Coast Inn and he would sometimes take me to a nearby restaurant to watch the goldfish play in the fountain. (The irony of my fondness for Bill Stewart is that in the 1948 World Series he was the umpire who made the controversial call on the pickoff play at second base that cost Bob Feller and the Cleveland Indians the series opener. Dad at the time was a coach for Lou Boudreau and the Indians, who then went on to beat the Boston Braves (more irony) in the series, 4 - 2.

That's me being held by my big brother Bill, sitting next to my sister Bea and my younger brother Jim.

Another thing I remember about spring training in my pre-school years was that I started keeping score – the way you're really supposed to do it. In fact, I knew how to keep score before I could even write my name. Don't ask me how I learned to do it. I just knew how. It's like asking the kids of today how they know how to use all of these high tech computerized devices and the answer always is, "I don't know how I learned it. I just know it."

Spring training was so much fun. It was truly a family affair, although Dad always left Wilkinsburg to head south a month or so before the rest of us. Then Mother would pack us up. Me. And my brother Jim, who was next to me in age although he was eight years older. And my sister Bea, who was 14 years older and went with us until she went off to college. I don't ever remember my oldest brother Bill making the trip because he was already in college when I was born.

When it was time to leave on our trip, Mother would put the chains on the tires if there was still snow on the ground in Wilkinsburg, and off we'd go. There were no interstate highways in those days. And no specified routes. And not many indoor bathrooms. It would take us three days to make the trip from Wilkinsburg to St. Petersburg and we'd always spend the first night in Berkeley Springs, West Virginia, which had an inn which Mother loved with beautifully decorated antiques.

If one of the chains broke, or it was time to take the chains off as we left the snowy north behind, Mom did the job by herself. And if the windshield was covered with ice when it was time to start out in the morning, Mom would place her bare hands on the ice to melt it so she could see where we were going.

Jim and I always played games along the way to see who would be the first to see Spanish moss hanging from the trees down south, who would see the first palm tree, and who would see the first sign saying we were entering Florida. And we really loved reading aloud the Burma-Shave signs we passed along the highway: "Careful birds . . .these signs cost money. . .rest awhile. . .but don't get funny. Burma-Shave."

Dad was a perfect family man. Kind. Caring. Loving. Fun. Also a devout Methodist, who earned the baseball nickname "The Deacon." When the season's schedule permitted, and during the off-season, he and Mother sang in the choir at Mifflin Avenue United Methodist

Episcopal Church in Wilkinsburg. In fact they first met in the church as teenagers after Mother's family moved to Wilkinsburg from Akron, Ohio.

It's interesting that although I have autographs of dozens of famous baseball players, managers and coaches, the only autograph I have of my father is in the front of a church hymnal, which says, "This book belongs to William B. McKechnie." You can tell it really is his signature because of the small circle he always placed above the "i" in McKechnie.

After spring training we would return home to Wilkinsburg. We never lived in Boston but Dad would always arrange for us to visit him for two or three weeks at a time. And I particularly remember him taking me for rides in a paddleboat on the Charles River.

I also remember "The House by the Side of the Road," a restaurant located in a rural area outside of Boston. In the same general area a young lady named Grace Godwin lived in a cottage on Lake Boone with an older couple who were friends of my parents.

Grace was following in her father's footsteps as an artist and in the summer of 1937 we all spent a couple of weeks together in the cottage and Grace asked Mother if it was OK for me to pose for her so she could do my portrait.

Everything went fine until the day I slipped an olive into my mouth while I was posing – and then couldn't decide what to do with the pit. I certainly did not want to spit it on the floor so I waited until I thought Grace wasn't looking and then I slipped it out of my mouth and placed it on the pillow next to me.

A few days later Grace was done with the portrait – and it was awesome. Mother had it framed and today it hangs in the family room of the home where Ted and I live in Jacksonville, just the way Grace painted it, right down to the olive pit on the pillow next to me.

On the back of the portrait are Grace's hand-written words: "A portrait of Carol Anne McKechnie, whose vivacity and charm, even at this early age of five, makes a portrait painter realize how insufficient his work can be." Grace Godwin 1937.

I guess I grew up in an adult world but to me Daddy was Daddy and having him as my father was just a part of everyday life, no matter how well known he was in baseball and elsewhere. Sure, I knew Daddy was someone important. We lived in a big, fancy house and the passenger train, which normally rumbled through Wilkinsburg without stopping, would always make an exception if Daddy needed to get off or climb aboard.

But all of that was a long time ago and, as I mentioned earlier, most people today have no knowledge of how I grew up in a baseball family – nor have they ever even heard of someone named Bill McKechnie.

But every now and then there is an exception. A few years ago I became interested in raising basset hounds and I met a veterinarian in Jacksonville named Dr. Lawrence Barrett. At some point in our conversation he found out I was from Wilkinsburg, Pennsylvania, and he exclaimed, "You're from Bill McKechnie's hometown."

"That's correct," I replied.

"Did you ever meet him?" the doctor asked.

"Yes," I said, "I lived with him for 21 years."

2

The Move Across the Bay – From the Braves to the Reds

I was too young to pay any attention to it at the time, but in Dad's eight years as manager of the Boston Braves he never came close to the success he realized in leading the Pirates to the World Series championship in 1925 and the Cardinals to the National League pennant in 1928.

From 1930 to 1937, as I found out later, the best Dad could do was to lead the Braves twice to a fourth place finish and one year he was chosen National League Manager of the Year, which says something about the caliber of the players and the job he did in managing them.

How the Braves did was certainly important to Dad but what mattered much more to me at the time were such things as going to school with my brother Jim during spring training in St. Petersburg. It was an outdoor school and I vividly remember, at the age of three, learning the shapes and sounds of all the letters of the alphabet while sitting at one of the picnic tables in the sand while the older students were in class. I was a class of one – and I loved it!

I wasn't so fortunate a year and a half later. I started first grade in Wilkinsburg when I was five years old and three weeks later I came down with pneumonia. I was so ill I was unable to return to school for the rest of the school year.

I was really sick, so sick, in fact, that not only did I have three doctors but I also had three nurses who worked in shifts staying with me around the clock. Mother said she could hear me breathing when she was downstairs and I was in my bedroom on the second floor. One night the end seemed to be drawing near and one of the doctors told Mother and Dad, "If she makes it through tonight, she just might recover." Thank God, I made it.

I spent several months in bed and I'll always remember how kind Caleb (Socko) McCarey was to me. He had been Dad's clubhouse boy when Dad was manager of the Pirates in Pittsburgh and had grown close to the family. Every day Socko would come by to see me, and he taught me the names of all of the states and also the capitals of each state. Socko later became a major league scout. And, yes, I still remember everything he taught me. What's the capital of Montana? Helena. Look it up.

Bea and I and our brothers Bill (rear) and Jim in the early 1930s.

And I'll never forget lying there in bed with the radio turned on and being startled to hear the announcer report that "Manager Bill McKechnie has left the team in Chicago and is flying home to Pittsburgh to be with his critically ill daughter Carol, who has pneumonia."

By the spring of what should have been my first year in school I was starting to recover from my illness and Mother decided it might be good for me if we went to Florida a month before spring training started. Instead of staying at the West Coast Inn in St. Pete where we usually stayed, we stayed at the Sorreno Hotel. It was a beautiful place and one day, while Mother was sipping tea with some of the dowagers staying there, I wandered up the stairs to the mezzanine where I heard a string quartet playing some lovely music.

One of the musicians spotted me and when he came over, I told him, "I can sing. Would you like to hear me?"

"Sure," he replied. "What would you like to sing?"

"In My Sweet Little Alice Blue Gown," I told him. So the quartet struck up the tune and I sang the words. But that's not the end of the story.

Dad's tenure with the Braves ended when his contract expired at the close of the 1937 season. The Cincinnati Reds immediately pounced on his availability and signed him to a contract.

The first thing that meant for me was that spring training would be in Tampa, not St. Petersburg, with new places to see and the opportunity to meet new friends and new players and their families.

One of the many friends Dad made before he left Boston was Oscar Horton, who made a fortune manufacturing inner soles for men's shoes at his factory in Athol, Massachusetts. Mr. Horton was a huge baseball fan and landed a top job in the Braves' front office. He and his wife had no children and treated me as their own.

Several years later, after Dad had joined the Reds and Mr. Horton had joined the Braves, Mr. Horton and his wife were attending spring training in St. Petersburg and they thought it would be nice to invite us to come back across the bay and join them for dinner at, of all places, the Sorreno Hotel. I think it was the first time I ever wore a black dress and heels.

As we entered the hotel, I could not believe my ears. There on the stage in the dining room was the same quartet and as soon as they saw me they immediately started playing, "In My Sweet Little Alice Blue Gown." Then one of the members of the quartet came over and invited me to sing with them again. But I was older now – and more inhibited – and I politely declined the offer.

What I have never figured out was whether dinner that night at the Sorreno with the string quartet was entirely a coincidence. Or did the Hortons hear about my earlier experience with the quartet from someone (like my mother?) and decide to have some fun.

If you get the idea that spring training was never dull, you're right. And it didn't make any difference whether it was in St. Petersburg or Tampa.

The first thing I noticed was that unlike St. Petersburg, where the Braves stayed in the three-story West Coast Inn, the Reds stayed at the 19-story Floridan Hotel in Tampa. Mother talked Jim Pickard, the manager of the hotel, into putting an enclosed cabana on the roof complete with a solarium and a big wheel like a merry-go-round, which could be turned so that Mother was always facing the sun. Mr. Pickard's daughter, Maryjim, and I loved to spin the wheel, especially when Mother was on it.

And I'll never forget the "Goody Goody" drive-in, three short blocks from the hotel. The cook's name was Cicero and he made the best burgers and shakes in the world. My brother Jim and I would always have a hamburger with mustard and a chocolate milkshake. And, instead of tables, the "Goody Goody" had chairs with flip-down arms – like the ones we used to have in school.

I missed all of my friends from the Braves, and especially my "sweetheart" Al Lopez, when we moved across Tampa Bay for spring training in 1938. But the Reds had lots of new friends waiting on the other side.

Like Frank McCormick, the Reds first baseman, and his wife Vera. Frank was like a big brother to me, unlike my own older brother Bill, who was always teasing me and making my life miserable. Frank, who stood a towering 6-foot-4, was always so kind and gentle.

And I remember Johnny Vander Meer, not so much for his back-to-back no hitters, but because of his green shirt which I dearly loved. He promised he'd give it to me some day, but I never did get it. But Johnny and his wife Lois were a lot of fun. I'd tease Johnny and poke at him and then he'd chase me around the mezzanine of the hotel in Tampa.

I was only six years old when Johnny pitched his two no-hitters in 1938, my father's first season with the Reds. I was too young to realize the full significance of what Johnny had done – a feat that has never been equaled. But I remember coming into the kitchen the morning after he had pitched his second no-hitter in the first night game ever played at Brooklyn and how excited Mother was.

"Guess what? Guess what?" she kept yelling. "Johnny pitched another no-hitter last night." Just four days earlier he had pitched his first no-hitter against the Braves at Cincinnati.

Then there was Ernie (Schnozz) Lombardi. If Frank McCormick was big, Ernie was enormous, standing virtually as tall as McCormick and weighing in at 230 pounds or more, and with a nose to match, which explained his nickname. Ernie exuded a very rough exterior but he was really a cream puff – if you treated him right. If you didn't. . .

Well, there was the day when I thought I was being funny when I said to him, "I bet you could hit a home run just by using your nose for a bat." Ernie did not think that was the least bit funny and I had to run for my life. Fortunately for me, Ernie was very slow afoot and I lived to tell about it. But I'm still upset over being so unkind to someone who really was so nice and who meant so much to Dad and the team. In Dad's first season with the Reds in 1938, Ernie was named the National League's Most Valuable Player and in 1986 he was inducted into the Hall of Fame.

Ival Goodman was one of the Reds' outfielders and I remember seeing his wife one day and asking my mother, "Why is she so fat?" Mother quickly covered my mouth and explained in a hushed voice that Ival's wife was carrying a baby inside her – and that was my introduction to the "facts of life."

Reds' pitcher Paul Derringer and his wife introduced me to one of the finer things in life. They had a place at the beach during spring training and had a set of Kirk's Repoussee silver that so impressed me that I put it on my registry when I planned my first wedding many years later. The sterling silver is still in use today at the home Ted and I have in Jacksonville.

Another thing that stands out in my mind about that first year Dad was with the Reds was returning home to Wilkinsburg when spring training was over and listening to the Reds' games being broadcast on the radio.

Powel Crosley was the owner of the Reds and he had made a fortune in the automobile, broadcasting and consumer appliance fields. So we had a Crosley radio, a large piece of furniture that occupied part of the living room and we could hear all of the games direct from Station WSAI in Cincinnati. The announcers were Dick Bray and Red Barber and they were great fun.

As it turned out, that summer was Red's last as a Cincinnati announcer. Larry MacPhail lured him to Brooklyn with a huge bundle of money and the next year he started doing the Dodgers' games.

Mother really was upset and I remember her begging Red to stay in Cincinnati. And I knew I was going to miss him, too, and hearing him tell all about being in "the Cat Bird Seat."

Would Red have stayed if he had known how the Reds were going to do in 1939 and 1940? We'll never know. But he sure missed a lot of excitement.

3

"There's No Place Like First Place"

What Dad did with the Cincinnati Reds in 1938 and 1939 is hard to believe even to this day.

In 1937, while Dad was still with the Braves, the Reds

Sugar, our Chihuahua, and I join my sister Bea and Mother while Dad browses through a souvenir program of the World Champion Cincinnati Reds, which he managed in 1940.

finished dead last, winning just 56 games and finishing 40 games behind the National League winning New York Giants. Then Dad took over and in 1938 the Reds won 82 games (26 more than the year before) and finished just six games out of first place behind the Chicago Cubs.

Then, in 1939 the Reds won 97 games and captured the pennant by 4-1/2 games over the St. Louis Cardinals. The World Series against the New York Yankees was another story but let's take first things first and start with spring training.

The highlight of the spring was a boat trip from Miami to Havana to play three exhibition games against a Cuban All-Star team managed by Adolfo (Dolf) Luque, who had been an outstanding pitcher for the Reds from 1915 to 1929, winning 27 games with an ERA of 1.93 in 1923.

It was on the trip to Cuba that I made the mistake of poking fun at Ernie Lombardi's nose and he tried to chase me around the boat. A lot of the other players got sick from the rough water and Mother was terrified of losing her balance and falling down (or overboard).

Things calmed down as we entered the harbor at Havana and it was fun leaning over the railing and watching all of the kids on the dock diving into the water to retrieve coins being tossed overboard by the players and other passengers.

Havana itself was even more fun and we were treated to dining at a palatial mansion during the few days we were there. One afternoon Mother wanted to go to the five-and-ten and hailed a taxicab to take us there. But Mother did not speak Spanish and the cab driver did not speak English. No problem.

"Llévenos al cinco-y-diez" I told the driver and he

took us right to the five-and-ten. Mother was speechless. What she didn't know was that the tutor I had at the hotel in Tampa was also a Spanish teacher in high school and she had started to teach me some conversational Spanish.

One day we were taken on a tour and visited a Catholic church which had a turntable in it. If you had a baby you did not want, we were told, you could put the baby on the turntable and one of the Catholic nuns would swing the turntable around and take the child off your hands.

Hard to believe? So was the bolita pole which was carried down the center aisle of the church during the break between the religious services. The pole had numbers on it that you could select to place your bolita wager for the day.

Whether it was the spring training experience in Cuba, the managerial genius of Dad or the development and emergence of the players from the year before, the regular season of 1939 was one to be remembered.

As they say, "There's no place like first place" and as the season breezed along Cincinnati and its multitude of fans literally ate, slept and drank baseball.

I was now eight years old and I don't know how many games I saw that year, sitting in Box 252 on the third base side at Old Crosley Field when the Reds were at home, and going to see them when they were on the road and playing at Forbes Field in Pittsburgh, a mere 10 miles from where we lived in Wilkinsburg. Altogether I guess I saw 60 or 70 games that year.

When the Reds were playing at home in Cincinnati, Mother would load up the car and she and I would make the eight-hour drive from Wilkinsburg. Along the way, we'd always stop in Zanesville, Ohio, at a Dairy Del for ice cream and a milkshake. We'd also stop in Circleville, Ohio, which billed itself as "the pumpkin capital of the world," and had a mountain of pumpkins right in the heart of town to prove it when the weather started to cool a bit.

Once in a while my brother Jim would join Mother and me on the trip. But Jim was now a teenager and he spent most of the summer in the Reds' bullpen, both at home and on the road. He had his own glove and his own uniform with the number 1/2 on the back, which was increased to 3/4 the following year. Whenever Jim could, he'd help warm up the Reds' pitchers.

One of the joys of Dad's success with the Cincinnati Reds was meeting all of the famous faces who followed the team. Here I am with movie star George Raft (left) and Al Ritz of the Ritz Brothers comedy team.

When Mother and I were going to be in Cincinnati for a long home stand we'd stay at an apartment hotel called the Vernon Manor. The grounds surrounding the hotel always seemed to be covered with acorns and Eddie Myers and I had a wild time tossing them around and also pelting each other.

Eddie was the son of Billy Myers, the Reds' shortstop. Eddie and I were about the same age but he seemed to be only about half my size. That figured because his father was only 5-8 – yet managed to hit .291 and nine home runs during the season.

For shorter home stands, we'd stay at the Netherland Plaza in downtown Cincinnati, which always fascinated me because it had the first enclosed shopping mall I'd ever seen.

The Netherland also featured a Hall of Mirrors where I loved to play with my friends Jackie Turner, daughter of Reds' pitcher Jim Turner, and Janie Wilson, daughter of Jimmie Wilson, the Red's coach and fill-in catcher. One day (it may have been the following year), Billy Giles, the son of Warren Giles, the Reds' general manager, decided to join us. Billy was a true clone of his father, who was not known as the easiest person to deal with when things didn't go his way. For some reason Billy became very upset and Jackie, Janie and I decided to take matters into our own hands. We locked Billy in a closet and left him there.

Fortunately for all of us, someone discovered Billy and let him out – and he went on to become a key figure in bringing major league baseball to Houston and then becoming the owner of the Philadelphia Phillies in some of their wildest and most glorious years.

Sometimes, after an evening game in Cincinnati, we'd go to a late night dinner at the Beverly Hills nightclub where we'd often meet up with Walter and Margaret Keagy. They were friends of Mother and Dad from Pittsburgh and Margaret was the wildest Reds' fan I've ever known. In 52 years she never missed an opening day. Her husband was the chairman of a natural gas company and the epitome of culture and refinement. Walter favored Shakespeare over the Reds – but he never missed an Indy 500 on Memorial Day.

Margaret and Walter Keagy had plenty to cheer about during the regular season in 1939. Bucky Walters and Paul Derringer won 52 games between them and Bucky was named the National League's Most Valuable Player.

Frank McCormick batted .332 with 18 home runs and 128 runs batted in. Ival Goodman hit .323 and Ernie Lombardi followed up his MVP season of a year earlier by hitting .287 with 20 home runs and 85 RBIs.

And then came the World Series against the defending champion New York Yankees, who had swept the Chicago Cubs in four straight games the year before and beat the New York Giants in both 1936 and 1937. I didn't see the first two games of the series, which were played in New York, with the Yankees winning them both, 2-1 and 4-0. I did see the next two games in Cincinnati and as Yogi Berra said many years later, it was like deja vu all over again. The Yankees won 7-3 and 7-4 and the season was over.

The World Series was a crushing loss. And, as was feared, General Manager Warren Giles did not take the setback lightly. When the final game was over he called Dad into his office and closed the door. After what seemed like an eternity, Dad emerged as white as a sheet.

It was a sad end to what had been an incredible season. As everyone suffered over the cold winter months and pondered what went wrong, little did we know that the best was yet to come.

4

From Tragedy to Triumph

Dad's antidote to losing the World Series was to go hunting with some of his old friends. Hunting was Dad's release and therapy and for all I know it may have started in 1928 when Dad guided the St. Louis Cardinals to the National League pennant, only to lose the World Series to the Yankees – also in four straight games.

One of Dad's friends was Doc Kilgus from the Western Pennsylvania town of Ligonier. Doc had a hunting lodge and he and Dad would bag quail and squirrels and jackrabbits, but never anything larger. Dad had a workbench in the basement of our home, which he used to clean his catch, and no one could clean a quail faster than Dad. He was amazing.

Quail also was one of my favorite foods and I still love it. My brother Jim and I would hang the wish bone of each quail we devoured on our milk glass to see who ate the most. Jim always won.

Sometimes Dad would also go hunting in Florida with E. V. Babcock, a friend of his from Pittsburgh who owned land near Punta Gorda on Florida's West Coast. Mr. Babcock is credited with introducing Brahma cattle into Florida and his name remains on some of the land he owned to this day.

The hunting therapy must have worked for Dad, or maybe it was the hunting plus going to church with Mother and me and whoever else happened to be at home on any given Sunday. For some reason we were always late for church, and Mother and Dad no longer sang in the choir, but let the record show that we did go to church.

When spring training opened in March, Dad and the players were ready. The prevailing attitude seemed to be, "We won the pennant last year and we can do it again this year. Only this year we're going to go all the way and also win the World Series. We're going to prove that 1939 was no flash in the pan."

It was fun seeing all of the players and coaches and their families again. And I can still remember standing in the lobby of the Floridan Hotel and looking up at the mezzanine where the players would congregate to play cards, smoke cigars and tell baseball stories.

When you'd see them up close I also remember how well dressed the players were in those days with their wing tip shoes; sport slacks, usually pleated; open collar, short sleeve sport shirts, and sport jackets which matched their slacks, with the collar of their sport shirts overlapping the collar of their jackets.

For me, spring training and the first several months of the regular season were nothing but a joy ride. Spring training in Tampa was lots of fun. I loved to help the maids at the Floridan Hotel clean the rooms, and the switchboard operators taught me how to plug and unplug the telephone lines, but they'd never let me talk on the switchboard phone.

The most fun of all was the day I punched out all of the numbers on the punchboard which sat next to the cash register at the newsstand in the lobby. At the time I had no idea that the punchboard was a form of gambling. For a dime (or maybe it was a quarter) you could punch out one of the 200 numbers. Your reward was a piece of paper which you unrolled to find out how much money you had won – if you were lucky enough to win anything at all.

I didn't know any of this on the day I became entranced by the punchboard and, when no one was looking, I proceeded to punch out all 200 numbers. Dad ended up paying for all 200, less whatever he won from some of the numbers I punched out. Suffice to say, I didn't do that again.

Dad fared much better when the regular season got into full swing. The lineup was pretty much the same as it was the year before. Ernie Lombardi was back as catcher and Frank McCormick was at first base and headed for another banner season. Lonnie Frey, Billy Myers and Bill Werber rounded out the infield at second base, shortstop and third base; Ival Goodman and Harry Craft resumed their outfield positions and Paul Derringer and Bucky Walters were poised to lead the pitching corps and win 20 games or more for the second straight year. The only real change in the lineup was in the outfield, where Mike McCormick (no relation to Frank) replaced Wally Berger, who was nearing retirement.

By early July the team had a secure grip on first place in front of the Brooklyn Dodgers and the St. Louis

Cardinals, and I remember what a wonderful time the players and everyone else had at the 4th of July party at the Country Club in Cincinnati. No one at the party, myself included, could ever have imagined the tragedy and the triumph that the second half of the season held in store.

Who's that next to me? It's Johnny Vander Meer of the Cincinnati Reds, the only pitcher in major league history ever to pitch back-to-back no-hit games.

For me, it all started innocently enough. One of Dad's coaches was Hank Gowdy, who first gained fame as a member of the 1914 Boston "Miracle Braves," batting .545 to lead his team to a startling sweep of the heavily favored Philadelphia Athletics in the World Series. Three years later, after the United States had entered World War I, Gowdy became famous again as the first major league player to enlist for active duty.

Hank and his wife had no children and Hank often took my brother Jim to the movies with him. By 1940 I was becoming of movie-going age myself and one day Hank invited me along to see "Four Feathers," one of the first Technicolor movies of all time.

I loved the movie but that night at the hotel in Cincinnati I got the chills and then developed a very high fever. Mother blamed it all on me being chilled by the new-fangled air conditioning system at the theatre. She called a doctor who came to the hotel and immediately diagnosed me as having a recurrence of my pneumonia.

Before he arranged for me to be admitted to a hospital, he told my mother, "A new miracle drug has just been discovered and I'd like to try it on Carol." And that, as I learned later, was how I came to be one of the first patients ever to be treated with a sulfa drug.

The drug may have helped but I still spent a week cooped up inside an oxygen tent and bored out of my mind. Finally, I got over the illness, thanks to the doctor and the good care I received at Cincinnati Children's Hospital.

But that was the end of my movie going for a long time to come. I didn't get to see "Dawn Patrol" with Hank and Jim (which I still regret) and Mother also would not let me or Jim go swimming in public for fear of catching polio – a frightening disease at the time.

But I still have a soft spot in my heart for Hank Gowdy. He had a very prominent dimple in his chin and he'd tease everyone and tell them it came from being struck by an enemy bullet during the war.

What happened to Willard Hershberger a short time later made my bout with pneumonia seem like nothing. Hershberger was the Reds' backup catcher behind Ernie Lombardi, and I remember how nice and polite he always was. He also seemed to be very popular with the other players and also with the fans, especially those of the opposite sex since he was single himself.

Hershberger got his big chance to play regularly in late July when Lombardi injured his foot. But things didn't go the way they were supposed to and there came a day at the end of the month when the Reds blew a three-run lead in the bottom of the ninth and lost, 5-4, to the Giants in New York.

Hershberger assumed all of the blame for the loss. "If Ernie had been catching, we wouldn't have lost," Hersherger was quoted as saying. "It's all my fault."

His teammates told Hershberger to forget it but things proceeded to get worse when the team went to Boston and two days later lost a doubleheader to the Braves, with Hershberger going hitless for the fourth and fifth time in six games even though he was still batting a very respectable .309.

Dad told us later that he noticed how depressed Hershberger was after the second game, so Dad asked Hershberger to have dinner with him that evening back at the hotel.

For the rest of his life, Dad refused to tell anyone what he and Hershberger talked about that night except to say that he did not get to bed himself until 5 o'clock in the morning.

Later on that morning, the players started to gather in the hotel lobby for the trip to the ballpark. Hershberger showed up and told them to go on without him and that he'd catch up with them later.

When it was time for the game to start, Hershberger was nowhere around. Someone called him in his room at the hotel and Hershberger's response was that he was too sick to play. He was urged to come to the park anyway. When he still failed to show up, Dad sent a friend of the team back to the hotel. A maid unlocked the door to the room and Hershberger was dead, his body slumped over the bathtub with his throat cut by a straight razor.

Dad was devastated. He knew that Hershberger's father had also committed suicide and now it had happened again.

The players were equally as devastated and many of them sobbed openly as grief overcame them. A few days later Dad called a team meeting and the players pledged to win the pennant for Hershberger and to give his mother a full share of their World Series earnings.

But things didn't get much better for the Reds in the days which immediately followed. Lombardi was still not fully up to strength but Dad had little choice but to ask him to return to his duties behind the plate.

As the days and weeks slid by, the team managed to maintain its hold on first place and the internal pressure on the players gradually eased off. And then, in mid-September, just a few weeks before the end of the season, Lombardi sprained his ankle and it seemed unlikely that he would play again during the rest of the season or in the World Series, if the Reds could hold off the Dodgers and the Cardinals.

Dad's only immediate choice as a replacement for Lombardi was 39-year-old Jimmie Wilson, a backup catcher for 16 years in the National League who now served the Reds primarily as a coach.

Dad asked Jimmie if he was willing to give it a try and Jimmie said yes. Somehow, Wilson helped Dad rekindle the team's spirit and more than adequately filled the bill as the team's catcher. When the regular season ended, the Reds were 12 games ahead of the second place Dodgers.

But for Wilson the season was really just getting started. What he – and the rest of the team – did against the Detroit Tigers in the World Series is, as they say, a whole other story.

5

"The Best Damn Manager in Baseball"

To say that Cincinnati was excited over the 1940 World Series against the Detroit Tigers would be a huge understatement. First, there really was not a whole lot else to get excited about in Cincinnati in 1940. And, second, this was another opportunity for the Reds to win the world championship – something the team had only done once before and that was in 1919 when the triumph over the Chicago White Sox was tainted by what later became known as the Black Sox scandal.

Forget about 1939 and being swept by the New York Yankees in the World Series. This was a new year and the Reds were going all the way.

The mood was temporarily dampened in the second inning of the series opener at Crosley Field in Cincinnati. The Tigers knocked Paul Derringer, the Reds' 20-game winner, out of the box with five runs en route to a 7-2 victory.

But spirits soared back up the next afternoon when 22-game winner Bucky Walters fired a three-hitter and the Reds won, 5-3.

Then it was on to the train for the trip to Detroit and Game 3. It's interesting to note that there were no days off between games in the 1940 World Series. Seven games. Seven days.

It's about 250 miles between Cincinnati and Detroit and that meant an overnight trip in a Pullman car. I had been on a train before but I'd never been on a train like this. What hoopla! The fans, the players and all aboard were totally upbeat and excited. I remember one of the players' wives – it may have been Vera McCormick, the wife of Frank McCormick, or maybe it was the wife of Ival Goodman – gave me her orchid to wear. Nearly all of the women were dressed up and wearing corsages. I mean, this was the World Series and we were in it!

I also remember the players, clustered in groups of four and five around makeshift tables in their Pullman cars, and playing Fan Tan – their favorite card game. The World Series? That was tomorrow.

In Detroit, we stayed and ate at the Book Cadillac Hotel downtown. There really wasn't any time for sight-seeing. By the time we got off the train and were taken to the hotel it was time to get to the ballpark. And the next two days were just as hectic.

The Tigers won the first game in Detroit, 7-4, to take a 2-1 lead in the series only to have the Reds fight right back and even things up the next day with Derringer rebounding from his first game problems and pitching the Reds to a 5-2 victory.

But the Tigers had their own fans to keep happy at home and Bobo Newsom, whose father had died just a few days earlier, pitched a three-hit shutout in Game 5 to put the Tigers back out front in the series, 3-2. And don't think the Tigers weren't a good team, with a lineup that included Hank Greenberg, Charlie Gehringer, Rudy York, Pinky Higgins and Birdie Tebbetts plus pitchers like Newsom, Schoolboy Rowe and Tommy Bridges.

But that didn't faze the Reds. The mood on the train trip back to Cincinnati was as upbeat as it had been on the trip northward a few days before. There didn't seem to be any apprehension. Everyone knew the facts. One more loss and the series was over. The Reds had to win two in a row. "No problem. We're going to win the World Series in honor of Willard Hershberger and also erase the memory of being blanked by the Yankees in 1939." That seemed to be the prevailing thought in everyone's mind.

When the train arrived in Cincinnati the station was jammed. There were people everywhere, yelling and cheering their heroes on to victory. Despite all the noise and bedlam, the fans up to this point actually were very well behaved. And no one during any of the games even poured a cold beer down my back as happened once during the regular season.

Moving up in the world. That's me on the shoulder of Powel Crosley, owner of the World Champion Cincinnati Reds, managed by Dad in 1940.

But there was no time to waste. Game 6 was that afternoon and Bucky Walters promptly evened the series at three games apiece by pitching a four-hit shutout.

That left it all up to Paul Derringer in the deciding game and Paul came through, with Jimmy Ripple driving in the tying run and Billy Myers' sacrifice fly scoring the winning run in the seventh inning. Derringer wrapped things up in the last two innings and the Reds held on for a 2-l victory. The dream had come true. The Reds had won the World Series.

When Paul recorded the final out there was instant pandemonium. I really can't remember much about it except how wild and wonderful it was. My brothers Bill and Jim were somewhere in the chaos down on the field. (My sister Bea missed the whole thing because she was in college at Penn State.) Mother and I were finally whisked away and escorted downtown to the Netherland Plaza, where there was even more excitement than there was at Crosley Field.

Ticker tape littered the streets and some exuberant fans even overturned a trolley car. Automobile horns were blaring and police finally had to close some of the downtown streets. It was wild!

Back at the ballpark, Dad was swamped with reporters in the Reds' dressing room and I still have a recording of one of the interviews in which he had high praise for Del Baker, the Detroit manager. But that was Dad, always finding something nice to say about everyone.

But who did Dad think was the best manager in baseball?

An hour or two later he and my brothers finally joined us at the hotel. That night we ate dinner in the hotel dining room with our friends Walter and Margaret Keagy. And I will never forget Dad standing up and waving a glass of Courvoisier and ginger ale and proclaiming:

"Walter, I'm the best damn manager in baseball!"

In my entire life it was the only word of profanity that I ever heard come out of Dad's mouth. And probably the only time I ever heard him pat himself on the back.

But Dad had lots to be proud of and he was the first to praise the players who made it all possible. Jimmie Wilson carried over into the World Series his inspirational performance as Ernie Lombardi's replacement behind the plate, guiding the Reds' pitching staff while hitting .353 and also stealing the only base for the Reds in the entire series.

Third baseman Bill Werber batted .370 and outfield

The smile of victory. Dad (above) with his arms wrapped around the commissioner of baseball, Judge Kenesaw Mountain Landis (left), and Warren Giles, the Reds' general manager, after defeating the Detroit Tigers in the final game of the 1940 World Series. Below, Dad shares his joy with his sons (and my brothers) Bill (left) and Jim.

replacements Jimmy Ripple and Mike McCormick batted .333 and .310. Frank McCormick, the National League's Most Valuable Player with a .309 batting average, 19 home runs and 127 runs batted in, managed to hit only .214 in the series with no homers and no RBIs.

But Frank's teammates, with Bucky Walters and Paul Derringer each winning two games, more than picked up the slack and that was all that counted. There was even a smile on the face of Warren Giles, the Reds' general manager, who had given Dad such a chewing out after the setback in the final game against the Yankees the year before.

Everyone was happy. Powel Crosley, the Reds' owner, was happy. Warren Giles was happy. Dad was happy. The players were happy. Mother was happy. My sister and brothers and I were happy. Cincinnati was happy.

The Reds were baseball's WORLD CHAMPIONS!!! My Dad was their manager! How lucky could an eight-year-old girl be?

6

Mother and Dad. . .
and the Good and the Bad

It's much more fun to talk about Dad and Mother than to recall the letdown the Reds suffered in 1941 after their glorious World Series triumph the year before.

If Dad was the "best damn manager in baseball" he was also the best father a girl could ever have. And Mother ranked right up there with him.

Dad was a "man's man." Dad loved hunting and he loved sports of all kinds, not just baseball but boxing, football and you name it. And he loved being around theater people – actors especially. Actresses? Well, maybe. But I never in my life saw Dad look at another woman.

Dad was a 33rd Degree Mason. His priorities were family, church and baseball. And, unlike Mother who was gregarious, outward going and upbeat, Dad was quiet. He had deep, deep feelings. And it really took something to make him express any emotion. Maybe some of that stemmed from the Scottish influence in his life.

Dad's mother and father both were from Glasgow and immigrated to this country and settled in Wilkinsburg.

Dad had eight brothers (three of them adopted) and four sisters. His middle name of Boyd came from the surname of his three adopted brothers.

As a boy Dad loved to swim in the nearby Monongahela River, which flows into the Allegheny River in downtown Pittsburgh to form the Ohio River. Dad also loved to visit the circus and water the elephants.

He got kicked out of school in the fifth grade when he brought a snake to school. And that was the end of his formal education and about the time he started playing baseball.

His mother didn't like baseball because he had to play on Sunday and that was against her religious belief. At the age of 17 Dad started getting paid to play and providing some family income. He broke in with Wheeling, West Virginia, in 1905 as a third baseman in the P.O.M. (Pennsylvania, Ohio, Maryland) League. And, believe it or not, I still have a picture postcard from Dad's memorabilia showing Dad with his teammates.

I sometimes think I was Dad's favorite. Dad was kind, and caring, and understanding, and he was always there when I needed him. Many years later when I told him I was going to get married, he broke down and cried and said, "I feel like I'm losing everything I ever had."

It was one of only four times I ever saw him cry. He also cried at Mother's funeral, at the close of my wedding ceremony – and on the day he spanked me. I had it coming.

I might have been three or four years old at the time and we had Sunday afternoon company at our house. I was playing by myself and found a "Tillie the Toiler" comic strip in the newspaper and next to it was the outline of a Tillie the Toiler paper doll. I asked someone to read me the directions, which said to cut out the outline, paste it on a piece of cardboard, and then cut it out again.

At first I couldn't find any cardboard. Then I remembered that my sister kept her high school senior class picture in her desk. When no one was looking, I took the picture, which had a cardboard feel to it, and pasted "Tillie the Toiler" on the back of the picture. Then I cut it out with a pair of scissors.

When Dad discovered what I had done to my sister's picture I got the spanking I deserved. Then he cuddled me in his arms and cried.

Mother and Dad, at age 56. Who could ask for anything more than parents like these?

From all I have read and been told about Dad over the years he was held in the same high regard by his players. His obituary in The New York Times on October 30, 1965 said, "McKechnie brought to managing a kindly air and a personality that wouldn't criticize, but rather helped."

Often referred to as "The Deacon" for his religious demeanor, Dad was described by baseball historian Lee Allen as "the sort of man that other decent men would want their sons to play for."

That was Dad. And Mother was the perfect match.

Mother, (her name was Beryl), was a rabid baseball fan and she and Dad were already going together in Wilkinsburg when Dad first started playing baseball. So she knew the game for as many years as Dad did and she was extremely loyal. She also never complained about

Dad's frequent road trips (or his hunting trips).

Mother was a true Christian lady and she and Dad first met at the United Methodist Episcopal Church in Wilkinsburg. She later served for several years as president of the Methodist Women's Society.

There wasn't much Mother couldn't do or wouldn't do, even if she didn't have to, and that included scrubbing the kitchen floor on her hands and knees even though we always had a live-in maid.

Mother (and Dad) both were wonderful cooks and Sunday dinner was always served promptly at noon – stewed chicken, mashed potatoes, yellow gravy, fresh green peas, coleslaw or homemade apple sauce, and yellow cake with chocolate icing or chocolate cake with white icing.

Mother also was always knitting or crocheting or quilting. And she also was the perfect host and our home was open to everyone – even to Uncle Joe, who was Dad's brother-in-law.

Joe was a roofer. He was always dirty. He also was near-sighted and when he'd stick his nose in a newspaper he'd put his glasses on the top of his head. He also had a wry sense of humor. One night when it was time for him to go home, he turned to Dad and said, "Well, I'm gonna do what the devil won't do. I'm gonna leave you now."

Despite her normal jovial nature, Mother suffered from one serious problem. She had postpartum psychosis which could cause her to have a nervous breakdown and become very anti-social and reclusive.

Mother was 44 when I was born and for the next year she was emotionally ill and she didn't get to hold me until I was a year old. But I had plenty of other "mothers" – aunts, cousins and, of course, my sister Bea.

What caused my mother's illness is hard to determine. Mother and Dad's first baby died when she was eight hours old. Or Mother's problem may have been related to her father's alcoholism although Mother never had a drink herself.

Mother's illness returned two more times during my life. But the mother I love to remember is the one who always told everyone how she "cleaned little white baby shoes for 20 years" – the length of time between my older brother Bill's birth and my graduation out of baby shoes..

Growing up with Mother and Dad was a joy. The same cannot be said for the Reds' season in 1941.

The team started out as world champions but nothing seemed to click. Part of the problem may have been the departure of Jimmie Wilson. After inspiring the Reds in 1940 with his stellar play late in the season and on into the World Series, Wilson left during the off-season to become the manager of the Chicago Cubs.

Not a single member of the team batted above .300 for the year. Mike McCormick hit .287, Frank McCormick fell to .269 and Ernie Lombardi had the poorest season of his career, batting just .264.

The outstanding player on the team was Elmer Riddle, a pitcher who won exactly one game in 1940. Dad moved him into the starting rotation and he proceeded to post an astonishing 19-4 record. Johnny Vander Meer regained some of the form he showed in 1938, with his back-to-back no-hitters, and Bucky Walters won 19 games. But Paul Derringer slid to 12-14, failing to win 20 games for the first time in four years.

When it was all over, the Reds still managed to win 88 games but could do no better than finish in third place behind the Dodgers and the Cardinals.

Most of the year's excitement was in the American League, where Joe DiMaggio hit safely in 56 consecutive games – a record that stands to this day. To go along with that, Ted Williams batted .406 for the season – and no one since has topped .400.

Ted also provided Dad with a personal memento. Dad was the National League manager in the 1941 All-Star game in Detroit because his team had won the league's pennant the year before.

All the National League had to do to win the game, 5-4, was to get one final out in the bottom of the ninth inning. Unfortunately for Dad and all National League fans, the next batter up was Williams – with two men on base.

Dad went out to the mound to talk to pitcher Claude Passeau. I never did ask Dad what they talked about or why they did not issue Williams an intentional base on balls and pitch to the less imposing Dom DiMaggio.

But for reasons never disclosed, Passeau pitched to Williams and Ted lined a shot onto the roof of Briggs Stadium for a 7-5 American League victory. Many fans still call it the most thrilling All-Star game ever played. Dad never revealed his opinion.

If there was one bright spot in the summer of 1941 it was my sister Bea's wedding on July 2, six days before the All-Star game. If my memory is correct, the Reds were in Pittsburgh for a series against the Pirates, so all of the players and coaches were on hand for the wedding along with all of our family members and friends.

In addition to the wedding, my mother's birthday was the following day. So there was plenty to celebrate. But what I remember most is how all of the players and coaches spent most of their time crammed into my "little cottage" playhouse in the yard outside our home. The playhouse had electricity and a radio, and the airwaves were packed with accounts of how Joe DiMaggio had just tied Willie Keeler's 43-year-old record by hitting in his 44th consecutive game.

Then, on the day of my sister's wedding, Joe broke the record by hitting a home run off Boston's Dick Newsome at Yankee Stadium. The players and, in fact, the whole country couldn't get enough of it. Joltin' Joe DiMaggio – who then went on to hit in 56 straight games.

It was fun being packed in my playhouse with all of the Reds' team members, including my old boyfriend Al Lopez, who now was one of Dad's coaches. I reminded him how he had "promised to wait for me" when I was a little girl at spring training.

But over all that happened in 1941, both good and bad, there was always the frightening spectre of war and the worry about whether our country would be drawn into the conflict raging around the world.

Baseball was a wonderful digression. But now the season was over and the long cold months of winter were beginning to settle in.

And then came Sunday, December 7, 1941.

7

Life and Baseball During World War II

Three days earlier I celebrated my 10th birthday. Now I was sick and lying in bed at our home in Wilkinsburg. I heard Dad coming up the stairs and entering my room. When I looked up he had this stricken look on his face.

"The Japanese have bombed Pearl Harbor. We're at war with Japan." I really didn't understand what Dad was talking about or all that it implied – what that fateful day meant for baseball, for our family, for the nation and for the world. Nothing would ever be the same again.

Lying there in bed I never could have imagined that my brother Jim would learn how to fly an airplane and become a bomber pilot. And I never could have imagined how his days in the Air Corps would somehow lead to the horrifying automobile accident involving my mother, Jim's fiancée Virginia, and me.

As the cold and dreary days slipped by in that fateful December, Dad could not help but wonder if he still had a job and what would become of baseball. The world was in chaos and winning the pennant was something less important than winning the war that engulfed us.

On January 15, 1942, many of Dad's questions were answered. In what has become known as his famous "Green Light Letter" to the commissioner of baseball, President Franklin Delano Roosevelt asked that organized baseball continue in spite of the war.

"I honestly feel that it would be best for the country to keep baseball going," the President wrote. "There will be fewer people unemployed and everybody will work longer hours and harder than ever before. . .If 300 teams use 5,000 or 6,000 players, these players are a definite recreational asset to at least 20,000,000 of their fellow citizens – and that in my judgment is thoroughly worthwhile."

So baseball continued in spite of the war and Dad continued as manager of the Cincinnati Reds. But everything was different. As major league players were drafted into the military to serve their country, the caliber of major league play diminished to that of AAA or AA, with older players and those unfit for military service filling the lineups.

The crowds diminished in size as more and more people put in extra long hours in the factories and mills to support the military effort. I remember going to one game in Cincinnati, maybe it was in 1943 or 1944, and the actual attendance was 139. I counted everyone who was there.

Night baseball became more and more popular as a source of relaxation for those who were wrapped up in their work during the daytime. And that was the thrust of President Roosevelt's thinking in his "Green Light Letter."

Spring training was another casualty of the war. Travel was restricted and gasoline was rationed so the major league teams trained in the north, using indoor facilities wherever they could be found.

The Reds trained in Bloomington, Indiana, at the University of Indiana, which had an indoor arena. If the weather was warm enough, Dad would take the team outside but usually it was too cold – or the snow was too deep.

Training indoors at the university did provide one unexpected bonus, however. One day one of the groundskeepers spotted this muscular guy taking batting practice for the university's baseball team. He called the player to the attention of Dad and Warren Giles, the Reds' general manager, who immediately signed the player to a $35,000 contract. His name was Ted Kluszewski and his biceps were so large that he had to have the sleeves of his uniform cut off at the shoulders.

"Big Klu" didn't break in with the Reds until after Dad was gone as manager but he became one of the most feared hitters in baseball – thanks to a very observant groundskeeper.

Spring training in the north also meant no more basking in the Florida sun each spring. Now I had to spend all year in school (sob!) and I was sick a lot with pneumonia and earaches.

The war affected everyone in the family. Mother knitted for the Red Cross and, like everyone else, she saved metal cans and grease and newspapers and rubber – anything that could be recycled and used in the war effort. Mother even made heavy wool soakers to replace the rubber pants that babies wore over their diapers.

My sister Bea spent the war with her husband Craig White, who became a Navy officer and was stationed at various locations in charge of physical fitness training.

My older brother Bill was involved in defense work in Maryland and my younger brother Jim, after graduating from Penn State, joined the Air Corps and became a B-25 pilot.

Dad continued to manage the Reds but the team just wasn't the same. After winning the World Series in 1940 and finishing third in 1941, the Reds finished fourth in 1942, second in 1943, third in 1944 and seventh in 1945.

During the war years, many of the regular players were called into military service and it was difficult for Dad and the other managers to patch together winning lineups. On the other hand, it opened the door for Pete Gray to play for the St. Louis Browns with only one arm, and for Joe Nuxhall to join the Reds at age 15 and become the youngest pitcher (and player) ever to appear in a major league game.

From what I've read, Joe threw his first pitch over the backstop, got two outs, walked five and gave up five runs. He didn't pitch in the major leagues again for eight years, when he returned to the Reds and went on to win 135 games. After that he became a highly popular broadcaster of Reds' games in Cincinnati.

I didn't get to see nearly as many games during the war years. Of course, I went to see the Reds play when they came to Pittsburgh. But gas rationing made it almost impossible to drive to Cincinnati and taking the train was more trouble than it was worth. Still there were some memorable moments during the war years, like the time I met the commissioner of baseball, Judge Kenesaw Mountain Landis. It was during spring training in 1942, the final year of training in Tampa until after the war, and Dad had been summoned to meet the commissioner in

Clearwater. For some unknown reason, Dad asked me to come along.

Judge Landis was known for striking fear in everyone he met with his fierce, unsmiling face. Everyone that is except Dad and me. Personally, I found him to be very nice. Mostly we talked about the war and the judge wanted to know what I thought. I told him, "As far as I can tell one of the big threats is the spying going on right here in our own country."

"Bill, what have you been telling her?" the judge asked my father.

Before Dad could answer I told him more about the U-boats being spotted offshore in the Atlantic Ocean and my fear of the undercover stuff going on all around us.

I was all of 10 years old at the time and what I told the judge came from what I had heard on the radio. But the judge seemed very impressed and we had a very nice lunch.

I still have no idea why he wanted to see Dad. The judge (and he really had been a judge) was probably in his late '80s but he still was the boss. Later I learned that his name – Kennesaw (with a second "n") Mountain – came from a Civil War battle near Atlanta in which his father was seriously wounded.

And then there was the night in 1943, when Branch Rickey came to our house for dinner. Mr. Rickey (my father always called him "Mister") was general manager of the Brooklyn Dodgers at the time and four years later was credited with spearheading the integration of major league baseball. After dinner, Mr. Rickey and Mother and Dad and I went out on the side porch and spent the next three hours listening to Mr. Rickey tell baseball stories in his very commanding voice. I was hypnotized.

In 1965, when Dad died, Mr. Rickey called and in a very faint voice apologized for not being able to attend the funeral because of his own illness. Three months later he was also gone.

Whenever we could, considering the travel restrictions, Mother and I would travel to New York when the Reds were playing the New York Giants or the Brooklyn Dodgers. We'd stay at either the McAlpin or the Roosevelt Hotel in midtown Manhattan and after a night game we'd always go to Dinty Moore's for something to eat. Sometimes Bill Terry, the former manager of the Giants and the National League's last .400 hitter, would join us along with his wife.

Dinty Moore, the owner, always came over to our table to talk. He had very large jowls and he was always very pleasant. The only problem with Dinty Moore and his restaurant was that Mother didn't like the prices. A piece of pie cost 50 cents!

The kitchen was open in full view and over in one corner of the dining area was an upright piano. One night an old-timer went over and started playing, and then another old-timer joined him and started singing along – "Swanee," "Rainbow 'Round My Shoulders," "Sonny Boy," "Mammy" – and all of the other old favorites. I remember thinking, "That guy singing is terrible." But I didn't tell anyone what I thought.

In a while the two came over and sat down at our table. The piano player was Ben Blue, a well known movie comedian who could also play the piano. The singer was a big baseball fan and a close friend of Dad.

It wasn't until a few years later, however, that I found out who the singer really was. In fact, Hollywood even made a movie about him – "The Jolson Story." I was glad I had kept my mouth shut when I heard him sing that night.

Dad even let Al Jolson sit in the dugout with him when the team was in New York. One day Dad told him, "My daughter is crazy about you and she would love to have you sign a ball for her." The ball is still part of my treasured memorabilia. On it is written, "To Carol, from Uncle Al Jolson."

So not all of my memories from the years of World War II are bad ones. But the one that stands out most clearly to this day was horrifying.

Mother and I and my brother Jim's fiancée Virginia were driving our big, old Cadillac from Pittsburgh to an Army Air Corps base in Georgia to see Jim get his pilot's wings.

It was mid-August 1944. The weather was beautiful but extremely hot. We had already spent one night on the road and were driving down this two-lane highway, heading toward our destination. Mother was driving; Virginia was in the right seat, and I was in the rear.

Suddenly this dalmatian ran out of a ditch right in front of the car. Mother hit the brakes and swerved the car. The dog panicked and ran in front of the car again. Mother swerved the other way, the brakes locked and the car careened off the road and crashed nose down into the ditch, partially lying on its left side.

I don't know how long we were trapped in the car. I vaguely remember hearing another car stop and two men carefully pulling us from the wreckage and slowly easing us into their car. Then they rushed us to a doctor in Fort Valley, Georgia. I still remember how wonderful the doctor was and the emergency care he provided. His last name was Kaye. Dr. Kaye.

It was a miracle we were still alive. Virginia had gone through the windshield and suffered a very large gouge out of her forehead and a severely lacerated knee.

Mother's glasses were shattered in the crash and the sharp pieces cut her around both eyes. Several of her ribs were broken and created intense pain with each breath she took.

The impact threw me forward and my face smashed into a metal bar on the back of the front seats. One of my teeth was knocked out and somehow fell into my hand; another tooth was left dangling out of my mouth, and the bones in my right cheek were crushed.

It's hard to believe that the two men who came to our rescue at the crash site waited while Dr. Kaye did all that he could for us. Then they drove us to a hospital in Macon. We owe the world – and perhaps our lives – to them and we never even got their names!

By the time we arrived at the hospital, the State Police had found out about the accident and notified Jim, who rushed from his base to be with us.

Poor mother. For three hours she had to sit on a three-legged stool in the emergency room waiting her turn to be treated. Then she was admitted to the hospital.

After Virginia and I were treated and released, Jim took us to a hotel in Macon. Dad arrived the next day and when he saw me he grabbed me and held me tightly in his arms.

The Air Corps put Jim on emergency leave and two or three days later he and Virginia and I took a train back home to Pittsburgh while Dad stayed with Mother in Macon. We had to change trains in Cincinnati and our friends, the Keagys, were at the station to meet us and offer their support.

I still remember the first meal we had on the train. Since I was missing two teeth and my face was such a mess, Jim cut my meal up into tiny pieces like it was baby food. Considering the shape I was in and the fact that I had barely eaten anything since before the accident, I think it was the best meal I ever ate.

Mother stayed in the hospital in Macon for a week or so and then Dad brought her back to Pittsburgh on the train.

I had never seen my mother so pitiful. She seemed to feel that everything was piling up on her. She would walk around the house crying but couldn't explain what was wrong.

My mother had been like this once before, right after I was born, but, of course, I couldn't remember that. Now I was 12 and everything had changed. I couldn't bring my friends to the house or do all of the other things I loved to do. I needed a mother but Mother would always be in a hospital in Pittsburgh, or New York, or be sobbing at home. I felt sorry for her but I missed her being the way I had always known her.

My father's sister and my mother's sister-in-law both stayed with us for awhile and we also had a housekeeper, who was not one of my favorite people. Things just were not the same and then, for some reason, it was decided that instead of going back to my old school I should go to Winchester Thurston, a private all-girls school, in Pittsburgh. To get there I had to take a bus and two streetcars during one of the snowiest winters I can remember.

For nearly a year and a half my mother suffered from her deep depression and then gradually she became her loving, friendly self again. World War II ended in August

Spring training with the Cincinnati Reds in Tampa, March 1946. That's mother and me and my sister Bea, with Dad holding Bea's daughter Sandra.

1945 and 1946 should have been a much better year. But it really wasn't.

Spring training returned to Tampa in 1946 and that's where Bucky Walters introduced me to a friend of his named Bobby Sprentall. Bobby was trying to make the team as an outfielder and I began to get the impression that he thought I was very nice. And I became very smitten with him.

One day he asked me to go to the movies with him – and that was the end of that. Dad stepped in and said that players were not allowed to date his daughter.As it turned out, that was also the end for Bobby Sprentall, who never did make the team.

The 1946 season also didn't turn out very well and the Reds finished sixth, 20 games under .500. Shortly after the season ended Dad was released after nine years as manager.

It was said that the fans forced the decision because they had grown tired of Dad's "old-fashioned" style of managing with so much emphasis placed on defense and pitching. The fans wanted more excitement. When Warren Giles, the Reds' general manager, let Dad go it was reported that he said, "Those fans just forced me to fire the best manager in baseball."

So what would Dad do now? And where would we go? The good news was that by now Mother had fully recovered from the automobile accident and I had returned to public school, which I very much preferred. It was the same high school in Wilkinsburg that my siblings, and also my mother, had attended.

But where would we go for spring training in 1947 and what would we do after that?

It didn't take long to find out.

8

Cowboys and Indians (Cleveland Style)

Not long after his release as manager of the Cincinnati Reds, Dad was asked to manage a team in the American League. Much to everyone's surprise, Dad said no.

He'd had his fill of managing. Not his fill of baseball. Just managing. More than 22 years as a National League manager was enough, with a track record that included four pennants and two World Series titles.

Dad was very comfortable with his decision. In fact, he even quit using his "Stay-in-the-League" hair spray that he had used to keep his hair black and keep him looking young while he was managing.

Now Dad had other things on his mind, like West Coast Marketing Corporation, a Florida venture in which he had invested with Jimmie Wilson – the same Jimmie Wilson who stepped in at the last minute as Ernie Lombardi's replacement and helped spark the Reds to their world championship victory over the Detroit Tigers in 1940.

West Coast Marketing owned acres and acres of citrus groves northwest of Bradenton, and acres and acres of land stretching from the Gulf of Mexico inland toward Bradenton, which were mainly used for growing tomatoes and green peppers.

Dad had also made the decision that we should sell our home in Wilkinsburg and take up residence in Bradenton. But things take time and I returned to school in Wilkinsburg to start my sophomore year in September 1946.

In December 1946 Dad went to baseball's annual winter meeting, as he always did, and when he came home he had a new job as a coach (not as the manager) of the Cleveland Indians, owned by Bill Veeck and managed by Lou Boudreau.

Veeck had acquired the Indians early in 1946 and Boudreau was the team's playing manager and shortstop at the ripe old age of 29. The Indians had finished sixth in 1946 but Veeck had bigger things in mind and Dad was hired to "help out" in running the team.

What a revelation all of this became.

First of all, spring training was not in Florida. Spring training meant the Cactus League in Arizona and learning to say "howdy" to all of the cowboys at the "Lazy V" dude ranch which Veeck owned outside of Tucson. There were 15 or 20 guests at the "Lazy V" including Boudreau, his wife Della and their three children. Boudreau was very friendly and easy to get along with and sometimes I would babysit for his two older daughters, Barbara and Sharon (who years later would marry Denny McLain, a 31-game winner with the Detroit Tigers in 1968).

The New York Giants trained in Phoenix and Horace Stoneham, the Giants' owner, had created a resort and every weekend we would go to a rodeo at a neighboring ranch called "El Jaffe," where we would enjoy an outdoor barbecue and doing Western dances and a Mexican Hat Dance. For a 15-year-old girl from Pennsylvania on her first visit to the great Southwest it was even more fun than baseball.

It was at "El Jaffe" that I met Rogers Hornsby, a Hall of Fame member and one of the greatest hitters in major league history, with a career batting average of .358. Veeck had asked Hornsby to coach the Indians' hitters during spring training.

Hornsby was a man of few words and, as I quickly found out, meeting him and really getting to know him were two entirely different matters.

Hornsby had a son named Bill and he and I went to the movies – once. Bill was very laid-back like his father and one date turned out to be enough.

During the spring someone bought our house in Wilkinsburg and when Dad went off to be with the Indians as the season opened, Mother put our household goods in storage and she and I moved into an efficiency apartment at the Penn Lincoln Hotel in Wilkinsburg.

After my sophomore year in school ended, I went to Pennington, New Jersey, to spend the summer with my sister Bea and her husband Craig, while Mother searched for a place for us to live in Bradenton.

During the summer Jimmie Wilson passed away and my brother Jim, who lived nearby in New York State, picked me up and we drove into Philadelphia for the funeral service. Jimmie, who was a native of Philadelphia, later was buried in Bradenton. Mother and Dad are also buried there and so is Hall of Famer Paul Waner.

Before the summer was over, Mother had found a two-story home on the Manatee River in Bradenton. I wouldn't say the home was large but years later it was converted into commercial office space.

It took a while to get the house set up and while Mother was busy with that and Dad was helping Lou Boudreau manage the Indians, I moved to Bradenton to begin my junior year in high school. Until Mother got everything settled, I stayed with Janie Wilson (Jimmie's daughter) and her mother. Janie was a year older than I was and she already drove a car – a green Oldsmobile convertible. The car had an automatic shift which allowed Janie to drive with her left foot sticking out of the wing window.

Janie was a joy. She'd bring a cup of coffee to me each morning while I was still in bed and she would also fix something to eat for her mother. After school, we'd get in her car and head to the "Cache" drive-in. We'd order a couple of Cokes while sitting in the convertible and wait for the guys to come by in their cars, honking their horns and waving and hollering at us.

It was a little hard for me to become accepted in school at first because not only was I someone new but I was also a Yankee – and this was 1947 and Bradenton and Florida were very much a part of the "old South."

Thankfully I had Janie and I also became friends with Dodi Manning and Betty Ann Merry (better known as Bam), who also came from elsewhere. We all became good friends and gradually things loosened up.

But the same cannot be said for Leola Saunders. Mother and Dad arrived in October, when the Indians' season was over, and we all moved into our Bradenton home.

Leola was Mother and Dad's housekeeper in Wilkinsburg and they brought her with them to Florida. That turned out to be a sad mistake. Leola was black. And the first thing that Mother and Dad learned was that Leola could not stay in the same motel with them on the trip south.

Nor was she welcomed by those she met in Bradenton. It all finally became too much and Leola had to return to Pennsylvania.

Much better news was the improvement shown by the Indians during the 1947 season. The team finished fourth but won 12 more games than it had in 1946. Bob Feller won 20 games, Boudreau and Dale Mitchell both batted over .300 and Joe Gordon hit 29 home runs.

It was nice to spend the winter going to school in the Florida sunshine and not have to put up with the snow and cold of Pennsylvania. Still, I couldn't wait for spring training in 1948 and a return to the wild west of Arizona.

Growing up. Here I am at spring training in Arizona in 1947. Dad was now a coach with the Cleveland Indians and I was becoming friends with Pete and Sissy Veeck, the children of Bill Veeck, the Indians' owner.

Dad bought me a frontier-riding suit complete with boots and a hat so I was all set for life back on the ranch. "Freckles" became my horse and every day Freckles and I would take a 26-mile ride into town and back over the "corduroy" trail to pick up the mail for the ranch. Dodo, Bill Veeck's sister-in-law, would join us on her horse and help to make sure we stayed on the trail and didn't wander off into the cholla – the painful, prickly cactus.

I also got to know Bill Veeck, the Indians' owner, personally. He had lost a leg during combat duty with the Marines in World War II and walked on crutches. But that never slowed him down. Not a bit. I found him to be very pleasant and fun to be around. He never wore a necktie, or a coat, or a long-sleeve shirt no matter how cold it was. He had kinky, blond, curly hair and a rugged but good-looking appearance.

Like Dad, he was a man's man. He knew what he wanted and he'd make up his own mind on how to go about getting it. As I found out, that did not always make him popular with baseball's other owners, but that never bothered him. Not Bill Veeck.

I think that maybe he saw dollar signs in Dad as a sort of behind-the-scenes manager while Boudreau made all of the visible decisions on the field from his shortstop position. Whatever the rationale, no one could ever question the results.

Spring training out west was as much fun in 1948 as it had been the year before but the best part came at the very end when the Indians played three games in Los Angeles against the Chicago White Sox before heading east to open the regular season.

One of the highlights of being in Los Angeles came when Mother invited me to go with her to a luncheon with some friends of hers at the Ambassador Hotel. We were in an elevator when two men also got aboard. One of the men was very frail and feeble and had to be helped with each step he took. I noticed that both men had camel's hair coats pulled over their shoulders, which seemed a little strange to me.

A few floors later the elevator stopped and both men slowly got off. When the door had closed, Mother looked at me very sadly and said, "That was Babe Ruth."

Mother had gotten to know him when Ruth joined the Boston Braves in 1935 while Dad was managing the team. The season had already started and Ruth played in only 29 games before deciding to bring his career to a close. He batted just .191 but one of his hits was his 714th home run – a major league record that stood for 39 years until it was broken by Hank Aaron in 1974.

When Mother and I saw Babe Ruth in the elevator he no longer was able to recognize her. And three months later, on June 16, 1948, he died. I wish I had known him.

Another highlight of our brief stay in Los Angeles was having dinner at Mrs. Moser's mansion in Beverly Hills. Mrs. Moser (I never did know her first name) was the mother of Laura Morehead, who had grown up with Mother in Wilkinsburg. Mrs. Moser's husband was deeply involved in drilling the nation's first oil well in Oil City, Pennsylvania, and later helped develop the oil industry in Oklahoma.

Laura was the matron of honor when Mother and Dad were married and later, when her own husband died, she stayed with us for a while in Wilkinsburg. I still remember that she took me into Pittsburgh to see my first opera ("Carmen") and also bought me my first sheet music (for "Oklahoma"). I still have a hand-painted powder bowl which she gave to Mother – three years before Mother and Dad were married. On the bottom it says, "LEM Christmas 1908."

When Laura found out that the Indians were going to be in Los Angeles for a few days she asked Mother and

Dad to invite some other members of the Indians' staff to have dinner at the mansion where Laura lived while caring for her mother, who was now in her '90s.

I remember Lou Boudreau was there, but not Della who had already left to take the children back to their hometown in Illinois. Among the others who were there was Oscar Melillo, another one of the Indians' coaches, along with his wife Ida. Spud Goldstein, the Indians' traveling secretary, was also there along with his two older brothers, Leonard and Bob Goldstein, who were in the process of creating Universal Studios.

After dinner, Dad asked me to entertain everyone by playing the piano and singing. When I was done, Spud Goldstein's brothers kept insisting that I should take a screen test and Mother proclaimed that I was destined to become another Deanna Durbin, a Hollywood actress and singer who shared the same birthday I did although she was a few years older.

To Mother, the screen test sounded like a golden opportunity and she was very disappointed when I turned down the offer. But I had absolutely no desire to be in movies. I loved theater and acting on stage but movies were a different matter. Plus I was afraid that movies would require a move to California and I was quite satisfied where I was.

So Mother was unhappy – and the evening was still not quite over. As everyone started to leave, Boudreau came up to me and gave me a "real" kiss on the lips. Then he turned to Dad and said, "Hey, Bill, how do you like this?"

The answer was that Dad did not like it at all. Boudreau's kiss was something more than just a brotherly hug. But Dad's anger didn't last long.

It was just about time for the team and all of the rest of us to pack our bags and head back east. The 1948 season was getting ready to begin. And what a season it would be!

9

Boudreau, Bearden – and Look Out Boston

Dad and Lou Boudreau had established a very close relationship during the 1947 season and it became even closer in the drama of 1948.

Dad always called Boudreau "Louie" and Boudreau always called Dad "Pops." In his book "Player-Manager," Boudreau said that Dad "has been like a baseball father to me."

During his 22-plus years as a manager, Dad always served as the third base coach as well. But with the Indians Dad spent most of his time in the dugout, counseling members of the pitching staff and, in general, doing whatever was necessary to keep things moving along smoothly.

That was no easy job in 1948. Bill Veeck wanted a winner and if the Indians were anything less it was no secret that Boudreau's job as manager was in serious jeopardy.

Despite a chilly temperature, 73,163 fans poured into Cleveland Stadium for the season's opener against the St. Louis Browns. The attendance was an opening day major league record and Bob Feller did not disappoint the crowd. Feller pitched a two-hitter and shut out the Browns, 4-0.

The Indians then proceeded to win their next five games as well and the American League pennant chase was on, with the Boston Red Sox, the New York Yankees and the Philadelphia Athletics all in hot pursuit.

I didn't get to see nearly as many of the games as I did when Dad was managing the Cincinnati Reds to the National League pennant in 1939 and to the World Series championship in 1940. When the 1948 spring training season was over out west, I had to return to school in Bradenton, which is more than 1,100 miles from Cleveland.

When Dad was managing the Reds we were still living in Wilkinsburg, which isn't all that far from Cincinnati. More than that, the Reds also played the Pirates in Pittsburgh and Forbes Field was just 15 minutes from our front door.

When my junior year in high school was over in June, I went to New Jersey to spend another summer with my sister Bea while Mother traveled with Dad. More than baseball, my big thing was sailboat racing and becoming the "Queen of Barnegat Bay." Bea's husband Craig was the skipper of a Lightning class sailboat named the "White Flash" and Bea and I were his crew. Every weekend we'd go to different yacht clubs at "the shore" (that's what they call the coastal area in New Jersey) for sailboat racing and parties.

As much fun as it was I never lost track of how the Indians were doing. According to the Sporting News, the American League standings on the morning of August 4 were "the tightest ever recorded in the history of the circuit at this stage of the season." The Indians were one game ahead of the Yankees, two games ahead of the Red Sox and three games ahead of the Athletics. The tension mounted with each passing day and I did get to Cleveland to see some games, if not as many as I had attended in Cincinnati.

Cleveland Stadium was something else. Unlike the friendly, but smaller, National League parks to which I'd grown accustomed, the home field of the Indians was a cavernous football-looking stadium sitting on the edge of Lake Erie.

I remember attending a night game when the stadium was invaded by "Canadian soldiers," inch-long green insects with wings, that were attracted by the lights and swept in off the lake. The swarms totally blanketed both players and fans until the game finally had to be stopped. Eventually the invasion let up and the game resumed but what a mess! There were millions of dead insects everywhere. Fortunately the insects were harmless but they were not exactly what Bill Veeck had in mind when it came to filling the stadium.

What Veeck had in mind, of course, were the fans and he knew how to draw them in record numbers by giving away nylon stockings to the women; flying in thousands of orchids from Hawaii; opening a nursery under the stands so that mothers could attend games; honoring "Mr. Average Fan" (Joe Earley) with gifts at home plate; having a special night and raising $40,000 for Indians' pitcher Don Black, who had suffered a cerebral hemorrhage, and adding to the pitching staff Satchel Paige, the legendary black pitcher from the Kansas City Monarchs.

When the regular season was over, 2,260,627 fans had seen the Indians in action, a major league record that was ultimately eclipsed by the Los Angeles Dodgers in 1962.

Paige was signed to a contract to do more than just attract fans. At the age of 41 (his "baseball age"), he could still pitch. In the last half of the season he posted a 6-1 record, which included two shutouts and an ERA of 2.47. More than that he allowed Bob Feller, Bob Lemon and Gene Bearden to catch their breath with an extra day off while they were on their way to earning 59 of the team's 97 victories.

Paige, however, did not break the color barrier in Cleveland. That distinction belonged to Larry Doby, who

Posing for posterity. Four key factors in the Cleveland Indians world championship season of 1948, (from left) starting pitcher Bob Feller; coach and former all-star Hank Greenberg; manager Lou Boudreau, and Dad, as coach and Lou's behind-the-scenes assistant. All four are now in baseball's Hall of Fame.

joined the team a year earlier although he managed a batting average of just .156. Amazingly, during spring training in 1948, Doby figured out how to hit major league pitching and he then proceeded to put together a .301 average during the regular season. He was joined in the outfield by Dale Mitchell, who hit .336, and by Thurman Tucker, Allie Clark and Walt Judnich, who shared the other outfield position.

But the Indians' real hero was Boudreau himself, who batted .355, drove in 106 runs and was named the league's Most Valuable Player. Boudreau was joined in the infield by Eddie Robinson, a solid performer at first base; second baseman Joe Gordon, who hit 32 home runs and drove in 124 runs, and third baseman Ken Keltner, who hit 31 home runs and drove in 119 runs. Jim Hegan was the catcher and his ability to handle the Indians' pitchers was far more important than his numbers at the plate.

So the lineup was loaded but so were the lineups of the Red Sox, with Ted Williams batting .369 with 25 home runs and 127 runs batted in, and the Yankees, with Joe DiMaggio hitting .320 with 39 homers and 155 RBIs. As the games dwindled down to a precious few, the Philadelphia Athletics slid out of contention and with just two games remaining the pennant was still up for grabs. On the next to last day of the season, the Red Sox eliminated the Yankees but the Indians won and were still one game out in front. All the Indians had to do was beat Detroit in the season finale in Cleveland. And then. . .

With a crowd of 74,191 on hand to watch the Indians win their first pennant since 1920, the Indians lost, 7-1, to pitcher Hal Newhouser and the Tigers while the Red Sox beat the Yankees again. The regular season had ended in a tie!

I could not believe what had happened. I was back in high school in Bradenton while both of the final games were being played. When school ended for the day, Janie Wilson and I raced home and she called the radio station to find out what had happened while I waited in suspense.

"Both games are over," she whispered to me with the phone at her ear, "and the Red Sox won."

"Surely, we won, too," I said breathlessly.

"No, the Indians lost," Janie responded.

"That can't be!" I screamed.

But it was true. A single game playoff was scheduled for Fenway Park in Boston and Boudreau and Bearden took matters into their own hands. Boudreau belted two home runs and Bearden, a rookie with the league's lowest ERA of 2.43, pitched a five-hitter. The Indians won their first pennant in 28 years, 8-3.

This time all of the guys in school were getting the score as the game progressed and I was exhilarated when the game was over. As soon my last class was finished I marched into the office of Mr. Davis, our principal, and told him, "I'm going to the World Series!"

"No, you're not," he answered.

"Oh, yes I am," I proclaimed. And that's just what I did.

Had the Red Sox won the playoff, the World Series would have been an all-Boston affair against the National League champion Braves. Now it was the Indians versus the Braves, who had become well known during the season for the phrase, "Spahn and Sain and pray for rain," which referred to their pitchers Warren Spahn and Johnny Sain, who had combined for 39 victories.

The first two games of the World Series were to be played in Boston and Mother and Dad were already there due to the playoff game. I flew to Boston with Max Cohen, who was with West Coast Marketing in Bradenton, Dad's off-season venture. Most of the flight was at night and I remember flying through a blizzard and everyone on the plane getting sick. Except me. I thought it was fun.

Mother and Dad met us at the airport in Boston and then it was on to the World Series. I was too young at the time to remember much about Boston when Dad was managing the Braves in the 1930s. So Braves Field was almost a new experience when we went to the first game, with Bob Feller pitching against Johnny Sain. Feller pitched a two-hitter and lost, 1-0.

It's how Feller lost that I'll never forget. In the eighth inning, the Braves' pinch runner Phil Masi got to second base following a walk and a sacrifice. When Masi made the mistake of wandering too far off base, Feller and Boudreau proceeded to work a pickoff play that they had mastered to perfection.

At precisely the right moment (after a silent signal), Boudreau snuck behind Masi and dashed for second base just as Feller wheeled and threw the ball. Startled by what was happening, Masi flung himself headfirst toward the bag just as Boudreau tagged him.

From where we sat (and photographs later proved) Masi was clearly out. But the umpire at second base called him safe. Two batters later, Tommy Holmes drilled a sharp single into left field and Masi raced home with the game's only run.

What hurt me most was that the umpire who called the play was Bill Stewart – the same Bill Stewart I remembered so fondly from those wonderful days of spring training when

I was a little girl and the players and the umpires all stayed at the West Coast Inn in St. Petersburg and he would take me to a nearby restaurant to watch the goldfish play in the fountain. I could not believe he made such a call in the World Series. And I still can't.

Bob Lemon evened the series the next day with a 4-1 win over Warren Spahn. Then, after an overnight train trip to Cleveland, Gene Bearden pitched a five-hit shutout for a 7-0 victory and Steve Gromek, the Indians "other" starter, rose to the occasion and pitched the Indians fourth complete game in a row for a 2-1 victory.

The next day a World Series record throng of 86,288 filled the seats to watch the Indians fulfill their mission. But things didn't turn out that way and the Indians lost, 11-5, when Feller was shelled in the seventh inning.

So then it was back on the train to return to Boston where the Indians won it all when Lemon and Bearden combined for a 4-3 victory.

I was elated but nothing in the World Series came close to the tension and excitement of the playoff game against the Red Sox. I do remember getting both a Boston Braves and a Cleveland Indians pennant as souvenirs while I was in Boston but for 30 years I never did anything with them.

Then one day in 1978 I heard that Warren Spahn was coming to Jacksonville (where I now lived) for a Little League function. I remembered the Boston Braves pennant and suddenly got the urge to have Spahn sign it. But I was teaching school at the time and also had a meeting that kept me from meeting him personally. So I asked my friend Connie Skinner, who was going to take her son to meet Spahn, if she would fill in for me.

I told her, "Just say 'Spahn and Sain and pray for rain,' and tell Spahn who my father was." Connie brought the pennant back with Spahn's signature on it. So now I have a bona fide memento of the 1948 World Series, signed by the opposition.

As soon as the '48 World Series was over I had to get back to school in Bradenton so I missed all of the excitement when the Indians returned to Cleveland to be greeted by an estimated 200,000 to 300,000 fans who packed the streets of downtown to welcome home the champions of the world.

For Dad it was world championship No. 3 to go along with his success with the Pittsburgh Pirates in 1925 and the Cincinnati Reds in 1940. Now he had risen to the top in the "other" league and done it as a coach rather than as a manager.

In his book "Player-Manager," Boudreau describes Dad's value to the team, especially in the tension-filled days near the end of the regular season when everything was at stake.

"Bill McKechnie, the dean of our coaching staff, was of inestimable value to me in those crucial days. Bill's help had always meant a great deal to me but never more than it did then. Wise in the ways of the world and of baseball, Pops kept me on an even keel. He was always there for me to lean on for advice, for consolation, for encouragement. I don't know what I would have done without him."

That was Dad. He was always there when you needed him most.

10

Cleveland...Boston... Cooperstown – and the Hall of Fame

After all of the excitement and success of the 1948 season, it's hard to explain what happened to the Indians in 1949.

The bats went silent and on the mound only Bob Lemon managed to win more than 15 games. Lemon posted 22 victories and the Indians did manage to finish with a respectable 89-65 record. But somehow the magic was gone. The Yankees won the pennant, the Red Sox finished second and shortly after the season ended Dad was gone.

Dad came home to Bradenton and West Coast Marketing Corporation and I packed up to go to college. I had always dreamed of going to Penn State, where my sister Bea and brothers Jim and Bill had gone.

When I was eight or nine years old, Mother insisted that Bea take me with her to a Fall Frolics weekend at Penn State. I suspect that Mother's motive was that if Bea had to look after me, she would not consume any alcoholic beverages, which was important to Mother since she was a teetotaler.

I won't give away any secrets but Bea and I did have a great time, especially being on hand to hear Benny Goodman and his band with Gene Krupa on the drums. A few years later, when Jim was going to Penn State, I also joined him for a weekend and it was just as much fun.

But now that it was my turn to go to college, Mother and Dad decided that the "baby" in the family was not allowed to stray that far from home. When Bea and Jim and Bill went to Penn State we were living in Wilkinsburg and Penn State was within about a three-hour drive.

Now we were in Bradenton and Penn State was well over a thousand miles away. So I wound up at Rollins College in Winter Park, Florida, near Orlando It took me about 24 hours after I arrived to realize that I had found a little bit of heaven at Rollins. And when I graduated four years later I sobbed uncontrollably at commencement even though I was getting married that very same evening. But that's getting ahead of the story.

Dad spent most of his time in 1950 and 1951 with West Coast Marketing and I can still see him inspecting the crops and stopping every now and then to pluck a tomato off the vine and seasoning it with the saltshaker he carried in his pocket before taking a bite.

After my freshman year at Rollins I spent another summer on the water with Bea's husband Craig, not at the shore but on Lake Erie near Buffalo. Craig had entered the "White Flash" in the Lightning class sailboat competition at the Canoe Club on Lake Erie. Bea had broken her arm and was unable to be a member of the crew, but as things turned out that didn't make any difference.

The weather was unbelievably hot, not a whisper of air was stirring, the lake was totally calm – and there was no sailing. So we just sat there, clustered together with all of the other boats and their crews, and a raucous good time was had by all.

And then, after another year at Rollins, it was back to baseball – not for Dad, but for me.

My brother Jim had joined radio station WENE in Binghamton, New York, and he was the announcer for all of the games of the Binghamton Triplets, a Yankee farm team in the Eastern League.

I spent the summer with Jim and his wife Virginia and after the games we'd go to Bill's Steak House for something to eat. After that we'd head to Paradise, a night spot in nearby Endicott which featured a wonderful piano player named Don Hickey and a drink called an "Ozark," which was a whiskey sour with a raw egg shaken up in it. I just loved my Ozarks and I spent the summer pouring them down until Mother and Dad paid us a visit.

Mother took one look at me and said to Jim's wife, "Virginia, Carol looks just wonderful! You've obviously been feeding her very well."

Between the whiskey sour and the eggs, my weight had jumped from 105 to 118 pounds. But I didn't dare tell Mother the truth.

In addition to drinking Ozarks, while I was in Binghamton I also worked part-time in women's sportswear at a department store in Endicott. And I got to hear Ella Fitzgerald and Louie Armstrong perform when they were in the area. So it was a super summer.

Then it was back to Rollins and in the spring of my third year Dad rejoined me in baseball, this time as a coach for the Boston Red Sox. Lou Boudreau was now managing the Red Sox (this was in 1952) and he asked

Dad to resume the relationship they had when both were with the Indians.

So Dad was back in the big leagues and I moved up a notch in the minors, joining Jim for another summer, but this time in Syracuse where he was with WSYR and was the announcer for the Chiefs, a Yankees' farm team in the International League. Mother and Dad did not know it at the time, but I also I dated a few baseball players, including Andy Carey, who went on to spend many years at third base for the Yankees.

But I had already found my true love during my sophomore year at Rollins. That's when I met Don Matchett. He was a year ahead of me in school and had come to Rollins on a football scholarship he had earned as an offensive/defensive lineman at Miami High School. As we got to know each other our relationship became more serious and we were finally pinned. Don was in Sigma Nu and I was in Alpha Phi.

Don graduated from Rollins in June of 1952 and went directly to the Navy's Officer Candidate School at Newport, Rhode Island. At Christmas time he came home and we visited Mother and Dad in Bradenton and Don's family in Miami, where we also got to see the Orange Bowl game. As a Valentine's present, Don gave me an engagement ring. We planned to be married in about a year, but the Korean War changed all of that when Don got orders to ship out on a six-month deployment with the Navy at the end of June. So we decided to get married on the evening of my graduation in the chapel at Rollins.

Dad was now in his second year with Lou Boudreau and the Red Sox and he arranged to take some time off so that he and Mother could attend the wedding on June 6, 1953. My sister Bea was matron of honor and my sister-in-law Virginia was the bridesmaid.

Don had to be back in Norfolk three days after the wedding so we spent the first night of our married life in Daytona Beach and the second night in Knoxville, before returning to Norfolk, where we stayed in a cute apartment on the beach facing Chesapeake Bay. I didn't have a clue what being a Navy wife was all about as I quickly discovered on my initial visits to the Officers' Club.

Three weeks later our honeymoon was over and Don shipped out as the gunnery officer on a destroyer.

With Don on the high seas, I went to Boston to stay with Mother at the Kenmore Hotel while Dad continued to help Boudreau manage the team. The hotel was within walking distance of the playing field and I fell in love with the coziness of Fenway "Pawk" (as it's called in Boston). Our seats were right behind the Red Sox dugout, where all of the wives and family members sat. And I can still hear a fan named "Lolly" ringing her cowbell. She was an institution at Fenway.

I also remember going to the hospitality room at Fenway with Dad one day and hearing Curt Gowdy, the well known Red Sox announcer, comment, "Doesn't McKechnie have a young wife?"

"That's not his wife," he was told. "That's McKechnie's daughter."

It's too bad the team didn't live up to its surroundings. The Sox were heading for a fourth place finish, 16 games behind the Yankees. Still, that was better than the year before, when Dad first joined the team, and the Sox finished sixth, 19 games back of the Yankees.

The biggest problem was the Korean War and the absence of Ted Williams from the lineup. Williams, who had seen duty as a Marine Corps pilot in World War II, was recalled to active duty to fly combat missions shortly after the start of the 1952 season and didn't rejoin the team until the final games of 1953.

At some point late in the 1953 season, Mother decided that we should take a break from the Red Sox and spend some time with Bea in Pennington, New Jersey. One Sunday afternoon we were listening to the Sox on the radio and a left-hander named Bill Henry was working on a no-hitter in the second game of a doubleheader when the telephone rang. It was Dad calling Mother to let her know that between games Lou Boudreau had told him that he was being released because he was too old.

We were all dumbfounded. Dad had just turned 67 but to all of us that was really not "too old." I never have found out who made the decision, whether it was Tom Yawkey, the Red Sox owner, or Joe Cronin, the general manager. I can't believe it came from Boudreau. But we all sensed that Dad's career in major league baseball was over after 46 years as a player and manager. (And Bill Henry, by the way, did not pitch a no-hitter that day.)

Mother and Dad retired to Bradenton and spent a quiet year until Mother's health started to deteriorate. Bea had a baby in August of 1954 and I had our first son, Stephen, three months later. The births triggered another depression in Mother much like the depression she suffered after the birth of each of her own children, as well as the depression she suffered after the serious automobile accident we were in.

Don and I were living in Bainbridge, Maryland, in the fall of '54 while he had shore duty, and I remember talking to Mother on the phone and thinking, "Oh, no, it's happened again."

Mother never really recovered and she died in Bradenton three years later, on October 26, 1957. Dad never left her the entire time.

When Don and I arrived at the funeral home for the viewing I begged him and Dad to let me wait outside. I was afraid of passing out if I saw Mother lying there. But Don and Dad were insistent and with one on either side of me they carried me inside. When I saw Mother she looked so beautiful and so peaceful. Until then, I thought it was better that her suffering was over. Now I wanted her back again.

The service itself was held at the funeral home because the Methodist church in Bradenton was not fully built. After Mother was laid to rest in the cemetery, Dad remained at her gravesite as everyone left. He just stood there, all by himself, alone with Mother one very last time.

Don and I enjoying our life together before he was diagnosed with Huntington's Disease.

I'll never forget her, singing every morning in the kitchen while she cooked or baked. She was so happy, and loving and nurturing when she was well. She loved children, and sewing, and going to church and keeping score during Dad's baseball games. She'd also get down on her hands and knees to scrub the floor or put the chains on the car in the wintertime. Mother did it all and I still love her and miss her.

Don and I had our second son, Kirk (which is Scottish for church), in January 1956, also at Bainbridge Naval Hospital. We were shocked at the cost. $10! When Stephen was born there it only cost $7.25.

The real shock came in April 1957 when Scott was born. Don had been discharged from the Navy and we were now living in Jacksonville. Scott was born at Baptist Hospital and the doctor's bill alone was $500 plus what we had to pay the hospital.

Don had a job as assistant personnel manager with Prudential Insurance Company which paid him a starting salary of $79 a week. Somehow we made it, while laying out $17 or $18 a week to feed ourselves, our three boys, and our fourth son David, who was born on July 25, 1961.

Enough to make a mother proud. Our four sons wishing everyone a Merry Christmas in 1961. From left that's David, Scott, Kirk and Steve.

After Mother's death, Dad returned to Bradenton and resumed his duties with West Coast Marketing while also traveling around the country to see his family members and friends. If he was going to pass through Jacksonville, he'd call us and say, "Meet me at the airport."

We'd pack up the boys and be on hand and Dad never disappointed us. He always had a brown paper bag full of coins for each of the boys, which they would then bring home and dump on the bed to count their riches.

We always spent Christmas with Dad in Bradenton and he'd have a Christmas tree hidden in the garage. On Christmas Eve, after the boys were asleep in bed, we'd all decorate the tree and put out the presents. Words can't describe the reaction of the boys when they awoke the next morning and discovered what Santa had done while they were asleep.

On Christmas day, Dad would bake bread and donuts in the oven and the aroma alone was worth the trip to Bradenton.

When Dad would visit us in Jacksonville, we'd go to the supermarket and he'd clean out the meat section, which meant that somehow I had to find a way to cram everything into the refrigerator. But Dad was such a joy.

One 4th of July weekend, when the boys were a little older, he went with us to see them in a Tadpole League game. Stephen was the pitcher, Kirk was the catcher, Scott played shortstop and David was the batboy. Dad sat there in the stands with all of the other parents and grandparents, cheering on the boys – and I don't think a single person knew who he was and that he had led two major league teams to world championships. That suited Dad just fine. He never sought attention. What mattered to Dad was that the boys and their team won, 4-2.

Back home in Wilkinsburg to cheer Bill Mazeroski and the Pittsburgh Pirates to their 1960 World Series victory over the New York Yankees. Around the table (from left) are my brother Jim's wife Virginia; my husband Don and yours truly; my sister Bea's daughters Sandy and Karen; Bea holding her baby daughter Claudia; Dad; my brother Bill; Bea's daughter Pamela; Bea's husband Craig and their daughter Leslie, and Jamie and his father (and my younger brother) Jim.

And who can ever forget Bill Mazeroski and 1960, when our hometown team, the Pittsburgh Pirates, won the National League pennant and had to play Mickey Mantle, Roger Maris and the mighty New York Yankees in the World Series? It was the first time the Pirates had been in the World Series since 1927 and the second time since Dad had managed the Pirates to a world championship in 1925.

The whole family went to Pittsburgh and we all stayed downtown at the William Penn Hotel. It was a wonderful excuse to get back home and revisit Wilkinsburg and it was fun to mingle with all of the players and former players and managers in the hotel lobby, especially Dad's friend Donie Bush, who managed the Pirates to their pennant in 1927.

The striking thing about Donie was that the lower half of his face was gone. I couldn't help but stare at it. "This is what chewing tobacco does to you," he explained to me.

Then turning to Dad, he added, "I sure wish I'd seen her when I was younger."

The first two games of the series were played in Pittsburgh, with the Yankees blasting the Pirates in the second game, 16-3. Then we all went to New York for the next three games. On the drive back to Pittsburgh for the rest of the series, our Buick station wagon developed problems on the Pennsylvania Turnpike and Don and I barely made it back.

When Dad found out what had happened, he took us to a Chevy dealer and told us to pick out what we wanted. We selected a red and white station wagon – and Dad insisted that he pick up the tab.

Because so many of our family members attended the World Series, we couldn't all sit together. During one of the games, a fan next to me saw me keeping score and said, "You seem to know a lot about baseball."

I thanked him for the compliment and told him I was the daughter of Bill McKechnie. "I've always wanted to meet him," the man said. So between innings Don and I took him to where Dad was sitting behind home plate and introduced him. The man was thrilled and we all returned to our seats.

More than 20 years later, in 1983 or 1984, our son Scott was handling reservations for Delta Airlines when he received a call from an older gentleman who said he wanted to make plane reservations so he could attend the World Series. The caller went on to explain that even though he now was blind, he always attended the World Series and would also need tickets for his personal aide.

As Scott took care of the details, he asked, "Did you happen to attend the 1960 World Series in Pittsburgh?" When the caller said he was there, Scott asked, "Have you ever heard of Bill McKechnie?"

"Bill McKechnie!" the caller exclaimed. "I sat next next to a young lady who was his daughter and she even took me to meet him."

"That was my mother," Scott said.

Bill Mazeroski's home run in the bottom of the ninth in Game 7 still leaves me grasping for words to describe the moment. The instant Mazeroski's bat hit the ball you knew the ball was going over the left field fence and the Pirates were world champions for the first time since Dad was their manager. By the time Mazeroski got to third base there was such a mob that I was afraid he'd never make it to home plate.

Pittsburgh erupted. The fans went bananas. I never experienced anything like it, not even when Dad's Reds beat the Tigers to win the World Series in 1940. It was a frenzy! Dad and Don and I tried to take a streetcar to Wilkinsburg but there was so much clutter and debris everywhere that the streetcar was stuck in its tracks.

Back home at Crosley Field, Dad throws out the first ball in the fourth game of the 1961 World Series between the Reds and the Yankees. Seated next to Dad is National League President Ford Frick. Despite Dad's pitching, the Yankees won the game, 7-0, and the World Series, 4-1.

Before we left the ballpark, Dad paid a visit to the dugouts. When he saw Casey Stengel, the Yankees' manager, he said, "We've been here before."

"Sure have," Stengel replied glumly.

The following year the Cincinnati Reds invited Dad to be an honored guest

Making it to the top. Baseball's Hall of Fame induction in 1962: Edd Roush (from left) with Jackie Robinson, Bob Feller and Dad, who looks like he might be weeping with joy.

at the 1961 World Series between the Reds and the New York Yankees. It was the first time the Reds, now managed by Fred Hutchinson, had won the National League pennant since Dad had led them to the world championship in 1940.

Dad asked me to join him so I left the boys with Don for a few days and flew to Cincinnati. Dad threw out the first ball in the fourth game at Crosley Field and made a good pitch, too. But the Yankees won the game, 7-0, and the World Series, 4-1.

That winter, in February 1962, Dad was visiting Jim and his family in Syracuse when the phone in the hallway rang. Jim's son Jamie answered it and came back into the living room and said, "There's a man on the phone who says he's Branch Rickey and he says he wants to talk with granddaddy."

When Dad rejoined everyone after taking the call, he said very quietly, "I'm in the hall."

"What hall?" Jamie asked. "You're in the living room."

"Not that hall," Dad said. "The Hall of Fame."

We all went to Cooperstown for Dad's induction into Baseball's Hall of Fame on July 2, 1962. Inducted along with Dad that day were Bob Feller, Jackie Robinson and Edd Roush, a National League outfielder for 15 years with a lifetime batting average of .323. Roush lived right around the corner from Dad in Bradenton and the two were teammates on the New York Giants in 1916.

Dad was sorry that Mother could not be there for his induction and his own reaction to being there was, "How can this possibly be?"

Dad had prepared nothing to say and when he was called on to speak, he wiped the tears from his eyes and said very solemnly, "Anything that I have contributed to baseball I have been repaid today, seventy times seven."

Celebrating Dad's induction into baseball's Hall of Fame are (back row, from left) my brother Bill's younger son Donnie; Paul Kerr, Hall of Fame publicity director; my husband Don; me and Dad, and (behind us) Jamie and his mother Virginia, the wife of my brother Jim. To the side of the plaque are my sister Bea, Bill's wife Peg and my brother Jim. In the front row are Bea's daughters Pamela, Leslie and Sandy.

11

The Second Time Around

A week after Dad's induction into the Hall of Fame, he attended an Old-Timers game at Yankee Stadium and then stopped in Jacksonville on his way back to Bradenton.

On Sunday, Dad and Don and our boys all went to Glynlea United Methodist Church and when Stacy Selph, our minister, spotted Dad he proceeded to tell the congregation, "That man sitting in the second row is the same one I saw on television at the Old Timers game at Yankee Stadium." He then went on to introduce Dad and talk about his induction into the Hall of Fame. It gave all of us a good feeling.

Dad's health gradually started to decline over the next year or two and it was determined that he had, what Dad described as, "a touch of leukemia." Dad joked about it and he still tried to lead a normal life, which, among other things, included mowing the huge lawn around his house no matter how hot it was.

When he was finished mowing he'd be soaked with

perspiration and to cool off he'd tilt his head back and pour a bottle of cold beer straight down his throat. No one ever understood how he did this. But as his illness progressed he found it harder and harder to do because of his difficulty in swallowing.

But Dad never lost his sense of humor. I remember visiting him in the summer of 1965 and how he told me, "I hope those snapping eyes of yours don't get you into trouble."

Dad continued to grow weaker and the chronic leukemia became more acute from a viral infection and then pneumonia. Dad died on October 29, 1965 at the age of 79.

His funeral service was held at Trinity United Methodist Church in Bradenton, where Mother, Dad and I were charter members. Many of baseball's famous names were in attendance, including Warren Giles, former National League president and general manager of the Cincinnati Reds. Al Lopez was there and so were Tony Cuccinello, Johnny Vander Meer, Paul Derringer, Bucky Walters, Billy Myers and many others of major league fame. Branch Rickey and Lou Boudreau were unable to attend the service but called to offer their condolences.

Dad was laid to rest next to Mother in Manasota Memorial Park just outside Bradenton. The cemetery is also the final resting place of fellow Hall of Fame member Paul Waner, and also of Dad's friend Jimmie Wilson and his wife as well as their son Bobby Wilson, who died during World War II, and their daughter Janie, who was my girlhood friend.

Now Dad was gone and there will never be another

like him. Even as I grew older, whenever he and I would cross a street together he'd always hold my hand. He was so loving. . .so caring. . .and straight as an arrow. With Dad everything was always black or it was white. There was no gray area in between. He was what his nickname implied. He was "The Deacon" – in church and out.

Each of us returned to our separate ways after Dad's passing. Jim went back to Syracuse where he was a radio and TV personality for many years. He later moved to Minneapolis, which is where he passed away, leaving two sons and two daughters born over a span of 31 years.

Bea and her husband Craig for many years lived in New Jersey where he had a chicken hatchery. When Craig retired they moved to Chiefland, Florida. Bea later returned to New Jersey after Craig's death to be closer to their five daughters.

My oldest brother Bill was the only one of Dad's four children to have a career in baseball. Bill never played the game because his hands were too small but that did not stop him from becoming the general manager of minor league teams in Birmingham, Trenton (when Willie Mays broke in) and Syracuse (before brother Jim became the announcer there).

Bill then went on to hold major positions in the farm systems of the Cincinnati Reds and the New York Giants. From there he became president of the Class D Florida State League before making a huge jump to president of the AAA Pacific Coast League.

When Bill retired from baseball he started a mobile home retirement park called "Hide-A-Way" in Chiefland, Florida (where Bea and Craig moved). Somehow, when Bill died, I wound up owning a couple of residences in the park, which I proceeded to sell. Bill and his wife Peg had two sons.

Don and I returned to Jacksonville and raising our four sons. Don continued with Prudential Insurance Company and over the next 30 years became assistant manager for Prudential's network of regional offices and also assistant manager of personnel.

Our boys kept growing and when David, our youngest, entered first grade I decided I needed to do something to keep from becoming bored. So I decided to become a teacher, which wasn't as easy as it sounds since I had been a theater major at Rollins. Before I entered the classroom I first earned a master's degree in education from Jacksonville University. Then I started teaching and kept at it for the next 31 years, mostly teaching at Fort Caroline Elementary School.

How many other boys grow up as grandsons of a Hall of Fame baseball manager? Here are my four sons in more recent years. From top left to lower right: Kirk, David, Scott and Steve.

We lived on Jacksonville's Southside for many years and every Sunday we'd go to the Glynlea Church where I sang in the church choir and sometimes sang solos, accompanying myself on the piano. Eventually we moved to University Park in the Arlington area of Jacksonville and became members of Arlington United Methodist Church.

As the boys grew older, one by one they started heading off to college and into their own careers. Our oldest son, Steve, wanted to be a baseball pitcher but an elbow injury in junior college put an end to that. Steve attended the University of Florida and today runs Mill Cove Golf Course in Jacksonville. Along the way, he owned several copy centers, served as a lobbyist, and also was in the swimming pool business. He has five daughters and is married to Jody, whom he met in church.

Although our second son, Kirk, looked more like his Hall of Fame grandfather than any of his brothers, he had no baseball aspirations of his own. Kirk was an engineering major at the University of Florida and helped start a Xerographic copy center and franchise operation in Gainesville. After he sold his interest, he worked with Steve at his copy centers in Jacksonville. A workaholic and a hands-on fixer of copy and reproduction equipment, Kirk now lives in Warner Robins, Georgia. He and his wife Lyn have two sons and a daughter.

Scott had dreams of a pro basketball career and still holds the record for assists at Florida Community College of Jacksonville (now Florida State College at Jacksonville). A walk-on at Florida State, he earned a basketball scholarship and later returned to Jacksonville where he taught math and was an assistant basketball coach at Terry Parker High School and head coach at Wolfson High School. Divorced many years ago, Scott has three daughters. He continues to live in Jacksonville and is suffering from Huntington's Disease, an hereditary illness that proved fatal to his father.

Like his brothers, David is a graduate of Terry Parker High School, where he won a baseball scholarship to attend Jacksonville University. But a shoulder problem ended his baseball dreams and he went to Gainesville and joined Steve and Kirk in the copy center business and later bought the Xerographic copy center in Jacksonville. He now co-owns DXM Marketing Group, a marketing enterprise with offices in Jacksonville and Savannah. He and his wife Jacqui have three daughters.

My husband Don had not reached his 60th birthday when a blood test first disclosed signs of Huntington's Disease, a brain disorder that leads to severe disabilities affecting the body, the mind and the emotions. Don's brother also had the disease, their mother had succumbed to it, and now our son Scott is suffering from the same illness.

Don's symptoms at first could hardly be noticed. But as the years passed his involuntary hand and arm and leg movements became more pronounced and his stumbling became more frequent. He finally had to retire from his position at Prudential Insurance and cut back on his bowling and golfing. He remained self-sufficient around the house but gradually that also began to taper off.

To have more time to care for Don I surrendered my role of teacher after 31enjoyable years. And then in the middle of a night in April 1997 Don fell in the bathroom and suffered a severe spinal cord injury which left him barely able to walk. The injury also damaged his vocal cords and created choking problems when he tried to swallow.

Don spent almost all of the next six and one-half years in the hospital or in bed at home, fighting severe bouts of aspiration pneumonia. After a few years I could not even help him shave or take a shower.

I don't know how I would have made it had it not been for Bobby and Stan Batten whom I had gotten to know while I volunteered in the gift shop at University (now Shands) Hospital. Bobby (that really is how she spelled her name) was a respiratory therapist and Stan was a locksmith and, even though they lived 35 miles away in Starke, they became like a part of our family, sometimes even spending the night or taking care of Don so I could go to choir practice.

One Friday morning Don became drenched in sweat. Bobby helped me dry him off but he became drenched again. Then I called my friend, Mary Browder, who was director of Medical Surgical Nursing at Baptist Medical Center, and she rushed to the house on her day off and our son Scott came home from school.

As Mary started to care for Don, Scott and I left the room for a few minutes. That was when Don breathed his last and his 15 years of suffering came to an end. On September 12, 2003, our 50 years of life and love were over. Don was 72 years old.

The memorial service was held at Arlington United Methodist Church five days later. In deference to Don's love for the Navy the service was conducted by Jack Hancy, a member of the church and a former Navy captain and chaplain. Jimtom Richardson, another church member, sang the Navy hymn. Our son Steve delivered most of the eulogy, assisted by Rusty Belcher, a minister and family friend.

Unable to attend the service were Ted Montgomery and his wife Jane, who was suffering from small cell cancer of the lungs. Ted and Jane had been friends of ours since we met at Glynlea United Methodist Church some 40 years earlier. They later moved to Arlington and joined the church there just as Don and I had done.

Ted and I with retired Pastor Stacy Selph on our wedding day, Nov. 12, 2005. Pastor Selph, whom we had known from our days together at Glynlea United Methodist Church in Jacksonville, married us at his retirement home in Lakeland, Florida.

Don and Ted were the best of friends. Ted was the pitcher and Don was the catcher on a slow pitch softball team and both also were Little League managers.

Six months after Don's death, Ted's wife Jane also passed away. After all that I had been through, my heart went out to Ted. He was an endocrinologist but don't ever think that doctors don't have feelings.

Ted and I obviously knew each other very well. Our kids had all grown up together and I had taught his two boys in the sixth grade. A year and a half after Jane died Ted and I decided that there was nothing to be gained by each of us leading a single and solitary life, so we were married on Nov. 12, 2005 and have lived happily ever since.

Since Ted was a doctor I decided that it might be a good idea if I could speak and understand his professional language. So I enrolled at a technical college and became a medical assistant, a position I filled until Ted and I both retired – but not totally. Ted still serves as a doctor and I serve as a medical assistant with Volunteers in Medicine, which assists the working uninsured in Jacksonville.

I also still have a reputation as a singer and piano player and have now been singing in a church choir since my early years as a teenager. I still find it hard to pick between acting, music, teaching and medicine. I just hope that isn't the Jill of all trades, master of none, syndrome.

Fortunately, Ted is a baseball fan so he's willing to put up with all of my memorabilia. And, yes, we do watch games on television and sometimes we go to St. Petersburg to watch the Tampa Bay Rays, especially when they are playing the Boston Red Sox since Jonathan Papelbon, the ace reliever of the Sox, grew up living next door to a physician friend of ours in Jacksonville.

And we go to Bradenton every now and then to watch a Pirates spring training game at McKechnie Field. In fact, I remember being there when they named the field for Dad shortly after his induction into the Hall of Fame. Ted and I always sit behind home plate with all of the scouts who use their radar guns to clock the speed of each pitch. Once we're seated, the first thing I always do is peer down the left field foul line and let my mind start wandering back in time.

When my brother Jim died in Minneapolis, his son Jamie took some of the ashes from his cremation and brought them to the ballpark in Bradenton, where he obtained permission to have a private, memorial service at home plate. But where to scatter the ashes? Jamie remembered his father telling him how as a boy growing up with Dad as a baseball manager, Dad would let him warm up the pitchers in the leftfield bull pen. So what better place to scatter his father's ashes at McKechnie Field?

When I look at the bull pen today my mind always returns to those wonderful years as "Daddy's girl" and growing up with one of baseball's most successful and best loved managers of all time.

Dad's name lives on at McKechnie Field in Bradenton, Florida, the spring training home of the Pittsburgh Pirates.

It really has been a pretty good life. . . even if no one today really believes that I am the daughter (and not the granddaughter) of Bill McKechnie.